BOARD N'STONES

About the Author and the Editor

Mr. Yasutoshi Yasuda

Born in Nakama, Fukuoka prefecture in 1964, Yasuda studied under Mr. Yusuda Oeda, a nine dan professional Go player, and succeeded in his aim of becoming a professional in 1985. He won the four dan section of the Kisei tournament in 1985. He was promoted to nine dan, the highest rank of professional players, in 1998.

Mr. Takeshi Yokouchi

Born in Nakano, Tokyo in 1962, Yokouchi joined the Yomiuri Newspaper Company in 1986. After working in the Niigata branch office and in the department of politics, he worked in the department of culture. He left the company in 1998 to become a freelance journalist focusing on mental problems. Since then he has focused on the effects of Go in both educational and therapeutic fields. He is the author of the book *Miracle Communication: The Magic Word of Go*.

Yasuda Yasutoshi

—

GO as communication

The Educational and Therapeutic Value of the Game of GO

BOARD N'STONES

『ふれあいの囲碁ゲーム–だれでもできるポン抜きゲーム』
Fureai no igo gēmu – dare demo dekiru ponnuki gēmu
by Yasuda Yasutoshi
Copyright © 2002 by Yasuda Yasutoshi
All Rights Reserved

Original Japanese edition edited by Takeshi Yokouchi and published by Tosho-bunka. The Japanese original has been rearranged and abridged with the author's permission for this publication.

The illustrations by Camille Lévêque are based on photos in the original Japanese edition.

The German National Library lists this publication in the Deutsche National-bibliografie; detailed bibliographic data are available in the Internet at https://dnb.dnb.de.

In accordance with Japanese custom and the usual order in East Asia, the family name always precedes the personal name in the case of person's names.

ISBN 978-3-940563-90-3

© 2021, BOARD N'STONES, Gunnar Dickfeld, Frankfurt a.M.
BOARD N'STONES is a trademark of Brett und Stein Verlag

Translation: Yoshimi Nakao
Cover design: Lars Decker
Illustrations: Camille Lévêque
Print: Books on Demand GmbH, Norderstedt

The diagrams in this book were created with SmartGo™: http://www.smartgo.com

Introduction

Go as Communication is the record of a surprising discovery, namely, that a simple game can have enormous educational and therapeutic value. The game of Go originated in China thousands of years ago. It is very popular in the Far East, and since its introduction to the West in the late nineteenth century it has slowly become more familiar to Westerners. The name "Go" is Japanese, and means "the surrounding game". The Chinese name of the game is "Weiqi"; Koreans call it "Baduk".

Yasutoshi Yasuda, the person responsible for this discovery, is a Japanese professional player. Concerned about social problems in Japanese schools, Yasuda began introducing the game to school children and discovered to his surprise that it had immediate positive effects. Children who were unruly became calmer and more interested in school generally; children who were withdrawn began to interact with others; children who were indifferent became animated. The effects were dramatic time after time.

Encouraged by these experiences with school children, Yasuda expanded his efforts to homes for the elderly and then to institutions for the mentally and physically handicapped. In every case, the game had tremendous positive effects. I can attest personally to the reality of these effects because I have accompanied Yasuda to a number of schools and institutions in Japan on two separate visits and I have taught the game to hundreds of school children in the US myself. Currently I am working with a group of mentally handicapped elderly people. Everything Yasuda says about the power of Go is true.

The version of the game that is used in these programs is quite easy to learn. Prior familiarity with Go is not required. There are more complicated versions of the game, but for these programs Yasuda uses a simple version called First Capture Go. Here are the rules:

The game is played on a grid of intersecting lines, 7 or 9 lines is a good size. The playing pieces are circular and of two contrasting colors, usually black and white, but any colors will do. They are played on the intersections and, after being placed, do not move.

You can play on any intersection, including on the edges. Here is a 9 line board with four pieces, called "stones", on it:

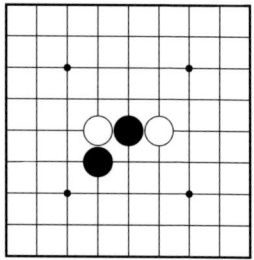

Black goes first, with the players taking turn about. The object is to surround one or more of the other player's stones by placing a stone on all the empty intersections it is touching.

In the next illustration, two black stones have been surrounded in this way. These stones, marked with triangles, are removed when their last empty intersection is covered, making White the winner because White has captured something first. [The Appendix in the book notes

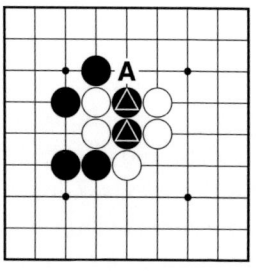

some possibly confusing situations that can arise in play. More information can be found on the Teaching Go page on the American Go Association's web site at www.usgo.org.]

This is a surprisingly interesting and challenging game, despite its simple rules.

Experienced Go players prefer to play a more complicated and challenging version of the game, and players of First Capture Go can easily progress to the more complicated version. I explain a straight-forward way to do that in *The Book of Go*, published by Sterling Publishing Co. in 2002, but any introductory book about Go will show you the difference. Many school programs that begin with First Capture Go later transition to regular Go, depending on the interests of the students and the intentions of the teacher.

A more challenging problem for people in the West who want to try out Yasuda's program is finding appropriate equipment, since Go sets are not as widely or cheaply available here as they are in the Far East. Happily, it is not difficult to make such equipment. For the playing sets a grid can be drawn on paper or cardboard.

Laminating a paper or card stock board makes a very durable set. The easiest way to create playing pieces is to put round self-adhesive labels on pennies. These labels can be obtained from any office supply store. For a 9×9 grid, 40 pieces of each color is a good number. Just make sure the grid and the playing pieces are of a compatible size – the "stones" should just touch each other as they are played.

When instructing a class and holding a team game with a sizable group, a larger board that can be fixed to a chalkboard is useful. The easiest way to make large "stones" is to attach small pieces of a magnetic strip to plastic poker chips. Then make a "board" of either paper or a thin plastic sheet with thin tape strips for lines and attach that to the board with some magnets. For very little investment you can have a nice demonstration board and plenty of sets for a large group.

There really is no impediment for anyone who finds this program as appealing – and inspiring – as I and many other people around the world do. The rewards are immediate and obvious. Scores of people in many different countries have introduced the capture game to thousands of people of all ages with very satisfying results. Yasuda's program offers everyone an opportunity to make a positive difference.

William Cobb
September 2002

Table of Contents

Preface

"You *are* a senile old man; you've forgotten to use your walking stick!"

We were playing a game of Go with the members of two teams taking turns placing a stone on the board at a day care center for the elderly. Suddenly, a man who had seemed able to walk only with the aid of a walking stick, stood up and walked toward me. He was so absorbed in playing Go, he had forgotten about his cane!

It is often said that people are losing heart nowadays. Am I the only one who feels that people, children and adults alike, look tired? I wanted to do something to help this situation, and a number of years ago I embarked on a plan of popularizing Go in the hope that I, as a professional Go player, could do something to help change society.

During the years since then, I have visited educational institutions, including preschools, elementary and junior high schools, as well as institutions for the mentally handicapped. The game I advocate is the capture version of Go, which does not involve complicated rules. In fact, anyone can enjoy the game by understanding a single, simple rule.

I've experienced amazing results. I have seen children and adults alike regain the sparkle in their eyes. The episode of the old man is but one example of unexpected results. I have often heard others call these miracles, but I would say that each of us has a great inherent power that is brought out through playing Go. At the same time, I am certain of the great potential contained within the game of Go.

Anyone can learn and enjoy playing Capture Go, since the game transcends age differences, disabilities, and language barriers. While communicating with others around the board, or when a group of players becomes united as one while playing a team game, we find ourselves enjoying interacting with others, leaving social status behind. In the process of considering the next move and discovering the right answer on our own, we realize our own great potential.

The Go program I initiated has spread throughout Japan and to schools and institutions abroad. During that time, I have reflected on the meaning of communication and interaction through Capture Go, and I have had so many moving experiences that I hoped I would one day be able to share with as many people as possible. I will be very happy if we can share the pleasure of Go through this book.

Yasutoshi Yasuda
January 2000

Yasutoshi Yasuda Teaching Capture Go to Children

Part One: The Impact of Playing Go

The Beginning – A Kindergarten in Shonai

It was around the beginning of 1993. I was only half watching the news on TV when a short item caught my attention: "A junior high school student playing in the gymnasium somehow caught his neck in a rope and died."

This so shocked me that I felt as if I had been hit on the head. How on earth could a boy of junior high school age be killed by playing with a rope? It had to be a case of bullying, which was becoming a serious problem in many schools. The boy must have been driven to suicide by being attacked by bullies. Surely anyone could see that. Why was the report presented the way it was? I sat upright and stared at the TV screen. Then, I heard a voice in my head, as if the boy was appealing to me, "There is something wrong with Japan."

A later follow-up item reported that a written note had been found, and it was determined that the boy had taken his own life. Could I let this current state of affairs continue? The voice crying out "Something is wrong!" could have come from my own heart.

In May of that year, my colleagues and I started a program to popularize the game of Go in schools. The objective we drew up for the program states that "Children are under tremendous stress nowadays. That stress has contributed to truancy problems and bullying. We want the virtues instilled through the game of Go to help nurture children's minds and enrich their lives." Many Go players supported this objective, and many students participated in this program voluntarily. However, our effort in popularizing the game didn't go as smoothly as we had hoped.

I still don't understand why I was so shocked by the news of bullying in the schools, or why I decided to start such a program all of a sudden. At some point, I became obsessed by the notion that I had to do something about the social problem in addition to simply popularizing Go. Sometime around then, I went to Shonai in Fukuoka prefecture to teach Go and met a member of the local Board of Education, Mr. Yoshihisa Ichiba. After the lesson, I talked with Mr. Ichiba, who was then head of the Instruction Division, and discussed with him my idea of eliminating bullying through the game of Go. I wanted Go to be included among classroom activities, not simply as a means of introducing the game, but to encourage the development of a sound heart and mind.

It may well have been a bit of a nuisance for him, being confronted with this out of the blue. Perhaps I rambled on a bit. It probably sounded like wishful thinking, trying to eliminate bullying through Go. It was an untested idea. All there was to go on was my sincere desire to eliminate bullying and to enrich the hearts and minds of children. More than anything else, what I wanted to do was to save even just one precious life.

Suicide notes left by children always say, "Father, Mother, I'm sorry that I could not talk to you about my problem." What if those parents and children had enjoyed playing Go, face to face? They might have developed an ability to converse with each other. Had the children been able to enjoy Go and use it as a means to communicate with friends and teachers, perhaps they would not have felt so isolated. Children need something that will bring them together, face to face. Thinking this, I just couldn't sit still. People around me, even my wife, thought I had gone crazy.

I asked Mr. Ichiba to recommend a Go program for the Shonai kindergarten. The reason I chose a kindergarten was because I felt that kindergarten age was the most important for the development of children's minds. Mr. Ichiba, who was familiar with Go, understood at once. Even with the support of the Board of Education, however, getting the teachers at the kindergarten to agree was another matter entirely. Each kindergarten has its own curriculum, and teachers there are extremely busy. Furthermore, they knew nothing about Go. "What are you talking about, when we are already so busy?" was apparently their initial reaction.

What do we normally associate with the game of Go? Just hearing the name, many people would likely think "a hobby for old men" or "something very difficult". Those teachers had no idea how Go and children could be connected together. Mr. Ichiba worked on the idea for a while, but the teachers started to walk away at even the mention of the word Go. At least that is what these same teachers later told me.

I could not wait indefinitely for a chance to try my ideas out on the teachers, so the only way left was to actually go directly there and make them listen, whether they wanted to or not. In May 1994, a happy coincidence brought such an opportunity about. Principals of public kindergartens are transferred every few years, and it so happened that at this time Mr. Terumi Tamura, who is a Go player, became principal of the Shonai Town Kindergarten. Mr. Ichiba talked about my idea to Mr. Tamura, and finally a visit to the kindergarten was arranged. The teachers agreed to give me two hours of their time after work one day.

The teachers there didn't know anything about Go, so they didn't know what to expect. It was obvious that they were not happy about staying late. It must also have been the first time they had met a Go professional, because until Mr. Ichiba introduced me to them they thought I was just the driver. They were surprised that I was so young!

Taking out the board, I spent only a minute explaining the game. What I said was "simply by surrounding your opponent's stone, you capture it." I was so eager to have them play that I didn't give them any difficult explanations of the more complicated rules, so we just started playing Capture Go, in which the first player to capture something wins the game. All the teachers enjoyed the games so much that two hours passed very quickly. This amazed even me, since I had not expected them to enjoy themselves that much.

At the end, I talked about my wish, that is, what brought me to the kindergarten. "I am not sure whether the children will take to it or not," I said, "but please at least introduce them to the game of Capture Go." Surprisingly, the teachers extended a warm welcoming hand. At the very least, they felt that five year olds could play the game.

The following day, the teachers began introducing Go to the children. Seeing a board on a table, some children gathered around and asked, "What's this?" The teacher simply said, "Put a stone down where two lines cross." On hearing that, a child put down a stone with a look of pleasure. Since the teacher knew the essential intent was "to surround and capture", she soon captured one of the stones placed by the children. The children were surprised. There was even a child who, having gone to the trouble of putting a stone down, grabbed the teacher's arm to prevent her taking it away again. Before long, one of the children realized that you could capture by surrounding your opponent's stones. The teacher at Shonai kindergarten had taught the children how to play Go without any explanation of the rules!

One month later, I visited the kindergarten. The teachers had apparently told the children that I was coming, and they were all ready to play Go with me. When I asked who wanted to play, a long line formed. We started the games with the rule: I win if I capture three stones, you win if you capture one.

I was surprised to see how well some children played. Until then, it was a commonly held belief that only a person who knew Go well could teach it. What I learned there was that a classroom teacher who knows nothing about Go is the best person to teach Capture Go to children. If a person knows Go very well, he or she would push students to learn more difficult rules, and the children would become confused and walk away. Even adults who are presented difficult concepts that they don't understand are soon put off, and this is even more so for children. Moreover, any tendency toward tedious explanations of the rules will make children hate the game. Looking back at my own failures in teaching and watching the teachers at the kindergarten, I realized what approach was called for.

Kindergarten children playing Capture Go

Since I knew I couldn't come to the kindergarten very often, I proposed that local Go players visit, but Mr. Tamura, the head of the kindergarten, rejected that proposal outright. "I understand your wish that we incorporate Go into our educational curriculum. However, this place is not a Go club," he stated bluntly. "Instructions in serious Go playing are not needed." Mr. Tamura well understood that Go is simply one of the tools to be used to help children. Looking back, I can see that without his decisive judgement, my program would not have been continued.

"People who don't know Go teaching Go" sounds like a cryptic remark from Zen Buddhism, but it's a vital point. The fact that I entrusted teaching Capture Go to teachers who had no previous knowledge of the game worked out well. Strangely enough, this has become a critical factor in Capture Go being accepted as an educational tool not only in Japan, but also all over the world.

Classroom teachers can grasp children's feelings and understand them well. To enjoy playing Go with children, to be on the same level where we can share the joy itself is good enough; complicated explanations are unnecessary. Despite a good knowledge of Go, the game will not succeed without an understanding of how children feel. What is important is neither technical knowledge nor Go skills, but a capacity to understand children.

At Shonai kindergarten, there was no specific period set aside for Go. Instead, they prepared Go game sets and left them for the children to spontaneously take up by themselves. The results surprised both the teachers and myself.

Go starts with a simple rule that five year olds can understand: Capturing a stone or a stone being captured. Children even enjoy it when they simply place a stone. What is so enjoyable about it? The teachers told me that one factor is the discovery or joy of finding out something for themselves. Go has infinite variations, so the same pattern will probably never be repeated. There are unlimited ways to capture and there are unlimited ways to protect. Each move is a step into an unknown world, and children play the game using total concentration of their powers of intuition and thought. Capturing and protecting are both discoveries. Come to think of it, we Go professionals do exactly the same.

The joy of discovery leads to an increase in confidence, which may then stimulate children's potential. They improve their abilities in various fields. These results led the teachers to believe that Go is a game that was different from other pastimes, one which has great potential for child development.

There was a mischievous kid called Ichan in the kindergarten. He was five years old, always had a runny nose, and did not get along well with the others. Ichan became interested in Go and started to play every morning with the principal of the kindergarten.

Ichan's playing became stronger and stronger, since he was playing with the principal regularly, and other children started telling him what a good player he was. The children had started to take notice of him. They had ignored his running nose before, but now started to tell him when his nose was running, and Ichan also became careful about wiping his face.

Ichan gained confidence by being accepted by his peers, and he found the will to try new challenges. He became able to put his shoes on by himself and also to use scissors, which he had not been good at before. Until then, he would just cut paper into pieces, but one day he made an elephant shaped bird's nest out of paper. "I hope a bird will fly into this bird's nest," he said. In no time Ichan became a leader in his class. The teachers were really surprised at this change in him, a change that also affected other children around him.

The following incident occurred near Shonai kindergarten one day. There is a children's recreation hall nearby that has Go sets provided, and elementary school children in higher grades were playing Go after school. Among them was a stronger player who was bossing his friends around, showing them how to play. Then along came some self-confident kindergarten children. Each kindergarten child played a game of Capture Go against the strongest boy, and they all beat him. The kindergarten kids then moved on to another game, leaving the boy agape.

The incident took place only a few months after they started playing Go at the kindergarten. Eventually not even the teachers could beat the children. It is amazing to find what great powers of concentration children have, and how flexible they are when they are having fun. A child's potential is much greater than what we as adults imagine. By pinning a label of immature on children, we may be missing something very important.

At the same time, the teachers were also making various discoveries for themselves. Mrs. Chiga Iwamura, a teacher at the Shonai kindergarten told me about one just the other day. Kindergartens contain materials for a large range of activities, such as drawing pictures or paper folding, but there is a decisive difference between Go and other activities. You start by sitting face to face with your opponent, and saying "*onegaishimasu*" [This phrase (oh-nay-guy-she-mas) expresses appreciation of the opponent's willingness to join you in playing a game], and when you finish you thank the other for the game.

Both players start together and finish together. After playing a game of Go, both children are satisfied with the game and start playing something else. When drawing pictures or folding paper, however, children all finish at different times. The children who have already finished will then ask others to play and those who do not complete the activity feel dissatisfied. However, all games of Go finish with some feeling of satisfaction for both parties. In another example, children tend to play with their favorite friends in a tight-knit group; and as a result, they get along only with these good friends. But after playing Go with different friends, the children often go off together to the playground to play. Thus relationships among children are expanded. A game of Go never has the same pattern, and therefore, children develop concentration while anticipating the opponent's moves. It seems that this kind of activity had not existed in children's education before.

The teachers also found their own human relations being expanded through Go. They were having as much fun as the children.

The value of educational activity through Go was presented to a children's education conference in Fukuoka prefecture. "There is no concrete data on this, but each child has become able to express their own opinion and listen to others' opinions. This change is amazing for five year old children," Mrs. Keiko Yamamoto reported.

The Alpine Go Village

After a Go program was established in the kindergarten in Shonai, another opportunity came to me. I was asked to introduce Go to the children in a municipal nursery in Omachi in Nagano prefecture. Led by the mayor, Mr. Yoshimasa Koshihara, Omachi was trying to invigorate the town by turning it into an "Alpine Go Village". One day, the mayor visited the Nihon Kiin, the Japanese Go Players' Association in Tokyo, to discuss putting this idea into practice, and I happened to meet him there. I talked about my experience at the kindergarten in Shonai and asked him to allow me to visit a nursery school in his city to try out my idea of a human development program. The mayor willingly agreed, and thus began my relationship with Omachi.

In August 1994, I visited Daisan nursery school in Omachi. I was again initially regarded as a nuisance, but this was understandable. It is a municipal nursery school, and they could not reject what the city office ordered. The teachers' reactions were familiar. "How could you come to teach Go at a busy time like this?" they said to me. When I explained my intentions, I noticed one teacher was nodding enthusiastically, but on closer inspection I found the teacher was actually nodding off! Perhaps since they had a preconception of Go as a dreary game, they weren't interested in me.

I finished the explanation anyway and decided to try playing Capture Go with thirty-five five year old children. The explanation was done in one minute: "Surround to capture." We started playing Go right away. As at the Shonai kindergarten, the children were soon enjoying playing the game, and the children's eyes lit up as they became totally absorbed. It was beyond the teachers' belief, and they finally realized that there is nothing difficult about playing Capture Go.

"I became convinced that this would work," said Mrs. Taeko Takizawa, the principal of the nursery school. Of course, Mrs. Takizawa had never played Go before. When she was asked by the city office to allow me to visit, she was very surprised, because she thought nursery schools had nothing to do with the "Alpine Go Village" idea. But what showed me that these are really professional educators is that the teachers were always thinking about what is most important for the children. After playing Go,

Nursery school children playing Capture Go

I talked with the teachers again, and this time, their attitude was completely different. When I talked about why Go is needed, it was Mrs. Takizawa who understood what I wanted to convey.

The change that occurred at Daisan nursery school was the same change I had observed at the Shonai kindergarten. In particular, the children's power of concentration was amazing. Children cannot sit still if they are bored, and the educators could not believe that those small children would sit still for thirty minutes or even an hour, concentrating on playing Go.

There was another positive result at Daisan nursery school. The children who learned to play Go talked about it to their families, and they started to play with their siblings and parents. This evoked a great response among parents. Mrs. Takizawa told me that some parents requested a Go meeting time when both children and parents could participate. Some parents made paper records of games to ask what moves they should have taken. Teachers there had never seen parents so positively involved. Not only that, but where three generations lived together in one household, grandfathers and grandmothers learned how to play Capture Go and were able to communicate better with grandchildren. Previously they had little opportunity for communicating with each other because of the generation gap, but now they enjoyed playing Go together. The story was broadcast as a feature program on a local TV channel.

Mrs. Takizawa explained it this way: "There are divisions in child education, such as music, language, exercise, health care. We guide children according to each of these divisions. However, Go doesn't fall into any particular category. Teaching or guidance involves the concept of educators providing a model example for the children to follow. With Go, however, children learn a simple rule and think of the next move while watching friends play. They can do it without a model. Until now there has been no other example of such a thing. It will lead to a revitalization of child education."

There is no fixed pattern of play in Go. It is a continuum of creativity and discovery. That is why there is no model. In the case of our own play, or in watching others play, we cannot move ahead without using our thinking faculties and creativity to the fullest extent. Even though I am a Go professional, I had never thought about it this way, and I found something refreshingly new in what I heard from Mrs. Takizawa.

The Go activity at Daisan nursery school has since spread to seven other nursery schools in the city. Lively expressions on children's faces make all of us happy.

In July 1995, there was a nationwide gathering of people involved with nursery schools and kindergartens that have incorporated Capture Go into their programs. It was the first meeting held under the title "Go Education". The results of the studies that were presented were all wonderful. The following is from the presentation by Daini nursery school in Omachi.

"Our experience with Go brought me to the realization that children have greater power to grow than adults imagine. I thought that there was no way a child could beat a parent, and that it would be unkind not to let them win. But now, however hard I try, I rarely beat my child. Although I feel somewhat vexed, at the same time I'm happy that I have been able to discover my child's potential.

"Nowadays children tend to watch TV and play computer games without having conversation with their parents. However, my children ask me to play Go with them. And I do so, and have conversations during a relaxing time at night or in spare moments while doing household chores. I'm sure that when they grow up, the children will remember this heartwarming, precious time they had when they were young. Also, every time I see a child playing Go with teachers at the nursery school, I think how lucky they are and appreciate the loving attention the teachers show them."

There were many similar stories. It is said that there is less communication between parents and children in today's society. It is also said that human relations are weakening. Go certainly makes the children come alive, but I felt particularly pleased that I had continued with the program when I learned that it was contributing to parent-child dialogue.

The word "Go" is a variant of the more common Japanese name for the game, which is *igo* and means "the surrounding game".

Go is also called *shudan* in Japanese, which literally means "hand talk" or "communication with the hands". It is heard to heart conversation without the need for words. Thus, communication is possible irrespective of age, gender, or nationality. Every time I read letters from mothers, I am impressed by the fact that people in the old days who used the word *shudan* knew that people could communicate through Go.

I also learned another wonder about the meaning of Go at the kindergarten. The following is from a letter from Mrs. Miwako Tanaka, a teacher at Daisan nursery school at that time: "I've realized that the origin of the name "Go" comes from the scene of everyone surrounding the board, thinking of the moves. I had first thought that the origin of the term was surrounding stones to capture, but how wonderful it is to see the scene that suggests the origin of the word. The children gathering around the board with their friends made this obvious. Next time I'm asked what Go is, I will able to answer with confidence. I realized that this was indeed the beginning of the interpersonal relationship that Mr. Yasuda had talked about. That is, the beginning of human relations, communication, and making friends."

I have still not forgotten the impact that this letter had on me. I had said repeatedly that Go is helpful for communication, but I had not reflected on that interpretation of the word, that people are connected with each other by surrounding a board. Until then, I had thought that as long as children enjoy themselves, it didn't really matter what they played. But on second thought, there is hardly any other game that one can enjoy on the same footing, regardless of age, gender, or language. Simply by surrounding the board, everyone can enjoy a common bond.

When I visited Daisan nursery school for the first time, I did not realize that there was a mentally disabled child among those thirty-five children two enjoyed Go. Later, one of the teachers said, "We've never seen her smiling so happily."

I knew that Go could be played by anyone and I had told that to everyone. However, I was not so confident that mentally handicapped children would be able to play it. In other words, I had no experience with such people. This incident at the nursery school gave me the idea to start knocking on the doors of institutions for the disabled. Incredible things awaited both myself and the staff at these facilities.

The Island of Nokonoshima

In Hakata Bay, Kyushu, lies a small island called Nokonoshima, on which live a total of around 900 people. It was, I think, the summer of 1994 when through an introduction from a friend, I visited the elementary and junior high schools on the island. Children at both schools enjoyed playing Capture Go, but the impression I received at the elementary school has remained particularly vivid.

The forty-odd pupils from the school all gathered together in one classroom, their faces full of curiosity about who was visiting them. There was, however, a hint of distrust or at least caution written on their faces. What I had to do first was to get them to trust me.

First, I had them introduce themselves and asked about their hopes or dreams for the future. As I had entered the classroom, one boy in particular had caught my attention. The boy expressed his defiance by leaning back on this chair. There was no change in his attitude when the teacher and I entered the room, and I sensed his obstinacy. Here we shall call this boy Kazuya. I asked him about his future.

"What do you want to become?"

"I want to be a professional soccer player."

"To become a professional soccer player, what do you need to do?"

"I want to become a professional soccer player if it's possible."

I spoke more loudly. "If it's possible? No one becomes a professional with such a tentative attitude. You shouldn't think of becoming a professional soccer player if you think that way. You should rather be thinking that where there's a will, there's a way."

Then I talked about how I became a professional Go player: "I learned how to play Go from my grandfather, and I was so fascinated by the game that I wanted to become a good player. Then my grandfather told me that my attitude should be to become the best Go player in the world. After that, I studied Go with that dream always in mind." Kazuya's expression changed somewhat.

During the thirty minutes of my talk, the children had begun to open up to me. Now was the time to introduce Go to them. We started playing immediately with the explanation of the rule: Surround to capture. Having decided that the capture of five stones would constitute a win, the games were over in no time. The children's faces were a study in delight as they stared at the board in contemplation.

Once the children got the hang of the game, we started a competition to decide the champion for each grade. Then each champion competed in a tournament. The other children cheered them on from both sides. People tend to think that Go is a silent game, but this is not true. When children play Go, the others all cheer their fellows on. "Not there!" they shout, "It's better here."

After a while, one of the boys came to me. "I'd like you to play with me," he said. It was Kazuya. As soon as I played Go with him, I realized that he had learned how to connect the stones in order to prevent them from being captured. I had only explained how to surround to capture and had not mentioned the tactic of connecting the stones. Kazuya had discovered this for himself. "You've learned a lot, Kazuya," I said, patting him on the shoulder, and Kazuya gave me a big smile.

One of the teachers later said to me, "We were really worried today, because there is one boy in the class who has a behavioral problem and we thought he might spoil the games." The boy she meant was Kazuya. Kazuya has many friends and takes good care of the younger students. However, he is hyper-sensitive and that makes it hard for him to conform to others' expectations. Adults often label this kind of child as a "behavioral problem". The encounter with Kazuya moved me and made me think more about children with behavioral problems, and this incident has become one of my cherished memories.

One day, I had an opportunity to talk with a young woman on a ferryboat to the island. There is a home for the seriously mentally disabled there called Himawari-no-sato, which she told me she worked for. I remembered well that when I visited Daisan nursery school in Omachi, there had been a mentally disabled child who started to show her feelings through her facial expressions during Go games. I handed my business card to the lady and tried to persuade her to introduce Capture Go at the home. I was sure they would get something out of it.

Such a suggestion out of the blue seemed to embarrass her. Her face looked as if she didn't have a clue what I was talking about. I couldn't persuade her any further and she never contacted me. Some time later, I asked to be allowed to visit the home through one of my acquaintances, but they gave me a diplomatic brush-off. Finally, however, in the fall of 1995, I was allowed to visit the home.

Mr. Hiroyasu Sakiyama, an old hand at the home, received me, but he seemed doubtful. He could not see how disabled people could possibly play Go. Why, not even he could play! I had initially encountered similar doubts from teaching staff at kindergartens and nursery schools, of course. I understood that no one was likely to welcome my idea of teaching Go to these disabled straight away.

Had I been asked whether I was confident about being able to teach them Go, I would have confessed that since I had no experience, I was not quite sure how it would go. I didn't have any concrete ideas on how to teach Go to them, either. I just prayed for a miracle.

Himawari-no-sato is a splendid two story house that is situated on the top of the island. Sixty people of all levels of disability live there. On that day, all sixty gathered in the cafeteria on the second floor, and I put up a large demonstration Go board.

On entering the home, I realized that the atmosphere was different from what I had imagined it would be. Some lay on the floor, some were running around the room, and others were screaming. However, the big hand they gave me had a warmth I had not experienced before. It was not polite applause for appearance's sake, but a genuine enthusiasm from within. I could feel that the welcome came from the bottom of their hearts. That relieved my apprehension, and I felt excited about the challenge ahead.

I do not explain the rule of "surround to capture" at these institutions immediately. Just placing a stone is a very hard task for them, never mind playing a game of Capture Go. As in kindergartens or other schools, we use a large Go board so that everyone can enjoy playing in the one game. Each person goes to the board to place a stone. All they have to do is place a stone on the board. Then the others give a round of applause to the player. At the home, even the shiest of people eventually became able to walk to the board, and each received a big hand.

After two or three turns, they got the hang of placing stones. Then an incredible thing happened. Their eyes started to sparkle. This amazed me as well as the teachers, including Mr. Sakiyama. Some of the residents are bedridden and have little facial expression, but those same people smiled and even walked and stood at the board. This seemed to defy accepted wisdom.

What a wonderful smile they showed every time they just placed a stone! Mr. Sakiyama told me that some often did not smile at a new teacher for several years. Therefore it was incredible to him that I had spent only one hour with them on the first visit, and yet they had such big smiles.

These homes for the disabled are isolated from the outside world in many ways. It could be said that the people who live in these homes are generally forgotten. The smiles of these "forgotten" people prompted Mr. Sakiyama to say that the recognition they receive through the applause of the others gives them a reason for their existence. In other words, the people who live in these homes want to be recognized. And once they are recognized, their hearts open up and joy is written on their faces.

We have seen how Go brought a sparkle to kindergarten and nursery school children's eyes. The same process was at work in the home for the mentally disabled, and both the teachers at the home and I have learned important things: We learned that it doesn't matter whether we can play Go well or not, what matters is whether we can communicate face to face on the same level. To "face" someone means that we think of the person as on the same level as ourselves. It means seeing a person as he or she is, without preconception or prejudice. This idea is not so hard to express, but in our own daily lives, how many of us sincerely face others square on? This principle has either been forgotten or is lacking in our daily lives.

After the disabled at the homes get accustomed to placing stones, I usually explain the rule "surround to capture". Some can understand the rule and some cannot, but I don't worry. *The purpose in popularizing Go is not to make good players, but to use Go as a means of communication.* I have the same purpose in mind whether visiting kindergartens, nursery schools, or homes like Himawari-no-sato. Therefore, the extent to which improvement in playing is achieved is not a matter of concern. If you can place a stone, and if it brings a sparkle to your eye, then the program has achieved its purpose.

Several months later, I revisited Himawari-no-sato. This time we were assigned a room rather than the cafeteria, and we tried playing Capture Go person to person. After a while, Mr. Sakiyama brought a young man to me and introduced him as their secret weapon. His name was Tsuru, and he was the same age as me. When I met Tsuru, he did not look at my face, which is always the case when he meets a stranger. As I addressed him, he dashed away. But he seemed interested in Go, and I soon realized that he was glancing at my play. I took him by the arm and sat him down opposite me for a game of Go. During the game, Tsuru never once looked up. I bent down to look into his face, but he turned his face away.

He was a very shy man, but when it came to playing Go, not only could he play well, he was such a good player that none of the teachers at Himawari-no-sato could beat him. As I patted him on the shoulder and told him he was great, he looked up for the first time and gave me a big smile. Of course the teachers were amazed since Tsuru never smiles until he comes to know a person very well. Later on, I was to learn a very important thing from Tsuru.

On my third visit to Himawari-no-sato, Tsuru played Go with someone else and so did I. Then I realized that Tsuru was trying to convey something to me, staring at my face. By this time, he had become a really good player, by far the best player at the home. As I looked at his board, it was his turn to move. He could capture his opponent's stones with his next move if he wanted to. He sent a silent message to me: "Can I capture these stones?" I didn't say anything but indicated an affirmative answer with my eyes, and he proceeded to capture them. We repeated the same thing three times. The fourth time, Tsuru didn't capture the stones, even though he knew he could. Instead, he put a stone down where his opponent could capture it. The opponent captured a stone for the first time and then ran around the room with joy. Seeing his opponent's joy, Tsuru also smiled. His face showed that he was very happy.

At that time, I had been thinking about what compassion for others is. I was not sure I really understood what the concept meant. Previously, I had discussed compassion with teachers at a nursery school, but we had not reached a definite conclusion. Since then, the words "compassion for others" had not left my mind. Now, what Tsuru had just done for his opponent and the word "compassion" linked up in my mind.

Everybody in the field of education says that compassion for others is very important, that we want children to grow up to be people who think of others, but what is compassion? Is being kind to people in difficulty compassion? In some cases this may be interpreted as forcing our kindness on other people. In other words, if we feel it is a burden to show kindness to a person, should we bear the burden merely to help them?

Tsuru's actions answered those questions for me. We feel happy in seeing others' happiness. Seeing their happiness, we share in it. Yes, sharing happiness. Since then, every time I talk about compassion, I tell the story of Tsuru, and I always find people agreeing with me.

We use the words "able-bodied" and "disabled". We pity the disabled and therefore feel we should try to do something for them. Disabled people do not want sympathy, however. On the contrary, they may even find our attempts very unhelpful. Even if we go to homes as volunteer workers, isn't it mere self-satisfaction if we think of ourselves as being more capable than they are?

Tsuru let his opponent capture his stones and seeing his opponent's joy, he also rejoiced. There was no superior attitude at being a good player, or of "letting" his opponent win. The compassion that Tsuru was far greater than ours. I have experienced similar cases at other homes. Is it right to call these people who as spiritually higher minded than us "disabled"?

The people at these homes are not capable of doing certain things. However, they possess in abundance the most essential human values such as kindness and consideration. I myself have been changed by them. It took a photograph to bring this change to my awareness. My colleagues had commented that they never saw me smiling. In this one photograph, however, taken while I played Go with the people at the home, I have a beautiful smile. I had never realized that I had such a smile. At the home, my role was to hand stones to the players. Each player came to the front to place a stone with such a happy smile on his or her face, that when I handed a stone to them, their warmth of heart must have been transmitted to me. Their joy energized me and washed away the negative notions in my mind.

I began to think that it would be a good idea if they could share their warm hearts and consideration for others with children at nursery schools and kindergartens. I felt that children needed to experience this while they were small, while their minds were still pure.

Eventually, a Go exchange was held between the oldest children at Noko nursery school and the residents at Himawari-no-sato. The nursery school children and the disabled played Capture Go with each other. As always, Tsuru put a stone where his opponent could capture it. Seizing the opportunity to capture the stone with his next move, the child ran around the room in delight, and seeing this, Tsuru was also happy.

In the beginning, however, the Go exchange between them did not go as smoothly as it does now. There were sixty participants from Himawari-no-sato and six children from the nursery school. When they gathered in the cafeteria, the children from the nursery school were tense. Some of the disabled lay on the floor and some screamed, and one of the children started to cry. I was concerned, but felt that I needed to keep things progressing. I divided them into several groups to play Go and put them in different rooms.

In no time, the children started enjoying the games and there was much laughter and noise. The children were sensitive enough to recognize that these people, although termed "disabled", have pure and warm hearts. After the games, the children and the residents enjoyed talking to each other and that amazed all of us. While it is sometimes three years before they will even greet a person, the residents were conversing happily with the children after just one game of Go. Go has also led to the formation of friendships between them.

A year later, another exchange was held between the two groups. The new children in the top level at the nursery school visited Himawari-no-sato for the first time. As in the previous year the children were tense. Himawari-no-sato has some seriously mentally disabled residents and among them was a young woman in a wheelchair. She was staring into space, with a blank look on her face. One of the girls from the nursery school went to the woman in the wheelchair and had her grasp a black stone. Then the girl supported the woman's arm and helped her place the stone on the board. The girl then put down a white stone. Again the girl supported the woman's arm and helped the woman put a black stone down, while she explained about surrounding stones. This was repeated several times. "She is smiling!" the girl suddenly exclaimed. The woman who normally showed little expression was actually smiling. Tears ran down my cheeks. The girl just wanted to play Go with her as another human being, and when the girl's feelings were conveyed to the woman she replied to it with her best smile. It was a memorable moment.

Touch is important for human beings. This does not necessarily mean physical touch, but rather a touching of hearts. The five year old girl showed us that what we adults must do is not just repeat slogans or theories, such as "thoughtfulness must be nurtured" or "foster a good mind". Rather we should create and nurture an environment where people can interact with each other. It is difficult to express in words all that I felt, but I was beginning to understand that communication as nurtured through Go might be much more powerful than even I had first thought.

Experiences at Anjaen

There is a home for the mentally disabled called Kasamatsu Anjaen in Shonai, Fukuoka prefecture. Anjaen houses one hundred people who are mildly disabled and whose ages range from eighteen to sixty. After gaining experience at other such centers, I was feeling more confident about introducing the program here. Through Mr. Ichiba, who had been the go-between for the activity at Shonai kindergarten, I asked the social welfare organization to be allowed to visit there, and Anjaen willingly offered me an invitation.

As is always the case, the staff were bewildered, since they held the common preconception that disabled people would not be able to play Go. I had grown used to that response, and it no longer bothered me. The people at Anjaen had a splendid time from the first day of the program. Since there were one hundred people there that day, it took a long time for each person's turn to come around. I visited Anjaen once every two months after that, which meant that those one hundred people had an opportunity to play Capture Go only once in two months, but even so I could tell that a gradual change had come over them. Applause from one hundred people sounds splendid and perhaps this helped to give each of them courage. Some of the people who had shown no interest in Go changed in no time. Some who at first placed stones in squares now learned to place them where lines cross, and they became able to capture stones by surrounding them. Not only have they become able to play Capture Go, but also their expressions have changed and their way of walking has become more confident and stable. Mr. Katsumi Yamasaki, chief instructor at Anjaen, who was unfamiliar with Go, could not believe that the disabled residents could change so fast.

There is a master Go player in Anjaen, whose name is Mr. Endo. While he knew how to play Go, since no staff members did, there was no opportunity for him to use his talent. Interestingly, after Anjaen introduced Go, he gradually shifted his position in the classroom. Mr. Endo was so shy that he sat at the back of the room at first. Over time, he started to take a chair closer to the front, eventually taking a seat in the front row. He started to show off, seeing that he had no rival when it came to playing Go. I spoke to him personally, pointing out that being a Go master, it is sometimes necessary to let the opponent win out of consideration for how the opponent feels. From then on, Mr. Endo started to sit where he was not conspicuous and to cheer on the others without pretension. The clothes he wears have also changed. At first he wore only dark colors, but now he wears bright colors, such as yellow shirts. He has gained in confidence. One day, he gave instructions as to where the chairs should be placed for the Go meeting. He was no longer the Mr. Endo that I had known!

A game on the demonstration board

In another case, a young woman with a timid attitude used to refuse to stand in front of others, but now on capturing a stone, she runs around the room with joy. Looking at each person, I recognized the process by which his or her appearance and behavior had changed. Success or failure is not so important, when loud applause and friendly laughter make us the hero or heroine of the moment. Being the center of attention for a moment removes the feeling of isolation, and this in turn may allow us to tackle new activities with enthusiasm.

On my visits to these homes, I realized that there are some disabled people who burst into rage or make strange noises. At first I did not understand what they wanted to convey through such behavior. It seems that our inability to understand what they want to convey creates misunderstanding and distance between us. Watching their outbursts during the games, I came to understand what they really meant, that this is their best way to express their joy.

When something unexpectedly delightful happens to us, we also make "strange" noises and leap for joy. Witness the way spectators rejoice over the long awaited score or goal at a baseball or soccer stadium. We tend to refrain from doing so under normal circumstances, however, worrying what others will think of us. Mentally disabled people are not likewise inhibited. If they are happy, they express their happiness using their whole body.

The disabled are bound by the name "institution" and the fences we construct around them, but they are also bound by the "fences" of our preconceptions and stereotypes. If it weren't for Go, I may never have come into contact with these people. Through my experience, I've realized that we need first to remove the fences. If we leave our preconceptions aside, we can discover the precious humanity that exists inside these people.

Now both the disabled people and the staff at Anjaen have changed. They have become cheerful and are willing to take part in various events that are held in the local community. Until then, to the local population Anjaen was just a home for the disabled in Shonai, and the local people's preconceptions and prejudice prevented them from seeing what was happening inside the facility. However, now that the disabled people are able to come out of the facility with confidence, the local population has also started to rid itself of prejudice against them.

Mrs. Masami Takeda, an instructor at Anjaen, commented that "not only have we taken part in various events in the local community, but also the local community has come to visit us. I'm very happy that the local people perceived what we really are and that I have come to know many people beyond the confined relationships within the home."

Anjaen is not the only such home that now enjoys exchanges with the local community. Exchanges where everyone can stand on the same footing, as human beings, are very different from ordinary visits out of sympathy or voluntary activity. Himawari-no-sato, situated on such a small island as Nokonoshima, was a peculiar existence in the minds of the local people. The home is on the top of a hill, and the local people used to think that it was dangerous for the disabled people to visit town; some even thought that, if they saw them on the outside, the disabled people must have escaped. However, none of the local people have those prejudices anymore. Through their interaction, they have begun to see disabled people in a different light. The islanders' attitudes toward the disabled are now full of warmth and friendship.

Mr. Yamasaki, from Anjaen, claims that "the change in the staff members' perceptions of the disabled has had a great influence on Anjaen. The introduction of Go to our home was the catalyst. Since then, both the staff, including myself, and the disabled residents have found our lives completely changed. This was totally unexpected. Go really does have a great deal of power."

On visiting many homes, I tell people that the disabled changed. Most interpret it as an improvement in the physical condition of the disabled, that they have somehow become closer to being "normal", but this is not exactly true. What I mean is that thanks to Go, their eyes have regained their natural sparkle. Of course there were physical changes such as people who seemed unable to walk who are now able to do so, and people who were very inward-looking becoming able to interact with others. However, the most significant change is that facial expressions have been enlivened, reflecting the change in the inner self. I think this must be the foremost reason for Go's acceptance in these homes. The disabled who lived such a monotonous life in a very limited space found that even such a life could be enjoyable.

Thus, I believe that it is important for us to enjoy our time together as human beings on an equal footing. It's easier said than done, because preconceptions and prejudice hinder us from doing so. Our social status, such as teacher or instructor may be another hindrance. Whether teacher, child, or the disabled, we are all the same human beings. Although we may understand this in theory, our attitudes might show us as looking down on them. Knowing just one aspect of them, we tend to label certain children as "behavioral problems" or people as "disabled" and this prevents us from opening their minds.

At kindergartens and nursery schools where the teachers do not have a superior or overbearing attitude, the children are very lively even without Go. Go may not be necessary if everyone can compete on the same level, and the teachers and the children enjoy themselves together. In my experience, however, I have found no substitute for Go. I couldn't agree more with Mr. Yamasaki's description of the "power" of Go.

A Class of Special Needs Children

Mr. Kiyoshi Yanagisawa, a former Japanese teacher at junior high school, is now engaged in popularizing Go in Hachinohe, Aomori prefecture. Mr. Yanagisawa believed in the positive power of Go and with this enthusiasm, he decided to take early retirement in order to pursue this goal. He learned of my program, and in the Fall of 1996, I was invited to his city. Go had been expanded from kindergarten into elementary schools and to a school for the deaf in the city, where later an unforgettable incident occurred. By that time, my program had been expanded to kindergartens, nursery schools, elementary schools and homes for the mentally disabled throughout Japan. This included classes for children with special needs, and schools for the disabled. Mr. Yanagisawa, being moved by my experiences with special needs children, took me to an elementary school in Hachinohe and asked me to play Go with the special needs children there.

In March of 1998, I visited the class for the first time. The principal told me that even though he had looked forward to the day, the children might not have the ability to learn Go. Entering the room, I saw eight children. Four children were sitting in the first row; the other four were sitting in the second row. Probably they were ordered to sit still by the teacher. As I spoke, they began to relax. Among them, there was a boy who kept putting his face down on the table. He had a tendency towards hyperactivity and sitting still must have been an ordeal for him. As I had them introduce themselves, the boy looked up suddenly and introduced himself, "I am Akira, and I'm in the fifth grade."

Before we begin Capture Go, I often write the kanji characters for Go on the blackboard and explain them to the children. One of the boys took out his notebook and wrote down these characters. Soon a page was full of the word "Go". As I patted him on the shoulder and praised him as a genius, he gave me a big smile.

As always, I started a capturing game with two teams. There was a small child, a first grader, who had Down's Syndrome. But when it was that small boy's turn to place a stone, after a long deliber-

ation, he placed a stone that captured five opposition stones. At that moment, everyone was so excited that they have him a big hand. The small boy skipped back to his chair happily. Then, Akira stopped him, patted him on the head and said, "You did a good job!".

An excited player

Later, I received letters from the children and the teachers. The children expressed the joy of having fun with the teachers and of having beaten them in the Go games. One of the teachers said that she was moved by that exchange and asked me to expand the program for the other children at her school. However, another teacher wrote that the special needs children have come to understand Go "at their own level". I could not forget the words "at their own level". As a Go professional, I judged that the children understood the game of Go much better than their teachers, but that was not the way that teacher saw the children. As long as a teacher has a preconception of the children as "disabled", he will not be able to seem them as they truly are.

At the end of June of the following year, I was invited to play Go with the ordinary fifth graders of the school. After we talked about their dreams for the future, the Capture Go competition started. Three classes were divided into six teams, three boys' teams and three girls' teams. The six teams and a teachers' team played against each other in a tournament. As is always the case, loud cheers could be heard all over the gymnasium.

The teachers' team won the championship on that day. As far as I know, it was the first time that a teachers' team won a championship. In the past, children always beat teachers. I know there is always an exception to any rule, but I was somewhat surprised. The children, though, took it for granted that the teachers would win.

This turned out to be the beginning of a drama. On that day, a team of special needs children was watching the games. When the tournament began, the special needs children asked me why they were not allowed to participate in the games. I told them in a small voice that they were so good that they were supposed to play later. Thus they waited their turn patiently. Of course, the teachers did not know that they were going to play with the special needs children later. The teachers must have felt relief now that they had won all their games. Then, through the microphone, I announced, "Now we are going to have a real final."

The team of special needs children came forward. The fifth graders cheered them on. One of the teachers dashed to me and told me that it was impossible for the special needs children to play Go. He was in charge of the special needs class, but he had been transferred to this school at the beginning of the new school year and did not know that the special needs children had played Capture Go with me three months before. I told him not to worry because they are geniuses and had the children come onto the stage.

The cheers from the fifth graders were nothing short of amazing, since the special needs children's team was now bravely playing a game against the teachers' team that even they could not beat. The fifth graders cheered them on at the top of their lungs, calling out their names.

The final game started. It is probably beyond your imagination how the game went. Some of the children lay on the floor, some danced, and some sang. The teachers looked very serious, contemplating their moves. A few minutes later, one of the special needs children captured more than ten stones! The fifth graders did not realize what had happened at first, and there was complete silence for a moment. In the next moment, the gymnasium was full of thunderous applause. Some punched their fists in the air; some shouted "hurray!" The fifth graders were as overjoyed as if they themselves had won the game. The special needs children also jumped with joy, but the teachers were dumbfounded.

Six months later, I made a third visit to the school. The children looked livelier than ever. They looked forward to having me play Capture Go with them. On that day, I took visitors from the United States and Germany with me. Each class welcomed them with songs and dances. I noticed that there was a girl that I had not met before. She was a first grader and was mildly autistic. During the game, the girl placed stones with happy smiles. Looking at her, the principal told me that he had never seen her smiling. In playing Go, her feelings were expressed spontaneously. Rather than worrying too much, it is important to create an enjoyable and relaxed atmosphere. Then everyone will smile spontaneously. Human beings are created to smile when we are happy.

Exchanges with a Day Care Center for the Elderly

Yuzamachi in Yamagata prefecture has been carrying out a campaign to improve community spirit from the standpoint of developing better relationships between people. The Go program was introduced there quite early on. Mr. Hideaki Sato, the agriculture instructor from the Japan Agriculture Association arranged my visit to the town. In October 1996, I visited the Fujisaki nursery school, which one of Mr. Sato's children attended. Mr. Sato had discussed my program with Mrs. Keiko Komatsu over the phone. Later, Mrs. Komatsu told us of the conversation, which made us burst into laughter.

At one end of the line, Mr. Sato said, "Why don't you try out Go at your school?", However, because of the local dialect, Mrs. Komatsu took it as "trying out the game of musical chairs". Until the day arrived, she never dreamed that they were actually going to play Go.

Yuzamachi and Szolnok in Hungary are sister cities, and there were many people from Hungary at the nursery school that day, about one hundred people in all including the children. The teachers had mistaken me for a translator. Therefore they looked unhappy when I did not translate even one word!

As we started playing, it became obvious that not only the children, but also the Hungarian adults loved playing Capture Go. As for the teachers, it was as if they had become obsessed with Go. Watching the scene, Mr. Sato was impressed and became certain that Go could be used as an instrument for developing relationships between people. Seeing children who cannot concentrate on anything for a long time sitting still for an hour and a half to play Go moved him. Moreover, he was impressed that everyone enjoyed the games together, transcending the language barrier and the generation gap. Thanks to the efforts of Mr. Sato, not only Yuzamachi, but other cities and towns in the vicinity have taken up Capture Go since then.

Up until this time, I had visited schools and social welfare homes, but no centers for the elderly. Mr. Sato asked me to visit a day care center for the elderly to play Go, because he thought that developing better human relations is important not only for children, but also for the elderly. Thus it was that I visited such a center in the Spring of 1996. That center for the elderly provides facilities such as a hot tub, and easy games for the purpose of keeping minds active. Elderly people in the area visit the center to relax and enjoy themselves.

It is often said that Go can help reduce age-related cognitive decline, but I had had no experience of teaching Go to the elderly and I was not sure whether I could get the same response that I got from children. In fact, I had no idea as to what I should say, but I decided to give it a try. There were both elderly men and women, seven in all. I supposed that there was no one who had played Go before, but I asked them to play with me anyway.

I took hold of the arm of an old lady who had refused to play and had her place a stone on the board. I told her to place a stone where the lines crossed and the others applauded her action. Each of them must have felt really happy in receiving applause, or perhaps just placing a stone made them feel like they were really playing Go. Their countenances became brighter, as if they had become children once again. Soon, they learned the principle of "surround to capture".

There was an old man who was at a more advanced stage of decline than the others. His mouth hung open and he would not move at all. I asked him to play and supported him to walk to the board at the front. However, he just stood still and would not do anything. I had him grasp a stone and supporting his arm, helped him to place it. Then the others gave him a big hand. Probably the big hand was a good stimulation for him. His mouth closed eventually, and with improved carriage he stared at the board in a contemplative manner. On about the third time round, the man, ignoring the correct order, walked briskly to the board. "You are a senile old man," I exclaimed without hesitation, "because you have forgotten to use your walking stick!" Everyone burst into laughter. Many of the elderly who visit that center use walking sticks and some are supported by staff members to stand in front of the Go board. Those same elderly people started walking on their own without help.

The elderly take turns visiting the center, and depending on where they live, they each have set days of the week on which to visit. I first visited the center on a Tuesday and it happened that later visits also fell on Tuesdays. By then, the players' faces were all familiar to me, but every time I visited the center, I repeated the same question: "Is there anyone who has not played Go before?" Without exception, everyone raised their hands.

As I continued, however, I realized that they had learned how to play. Every time I visit I find they have improved. The staff members of the center were in their 30's and 40's and yet when those young staff members played Capture Go with the elderly, they could not always beat them. Both the elderly people and the staff members thought about the next move seriously. It created a really good atmosphere. I started to think that the elderly should play Capture Go with children from a nursery school, since Go is an instrument for connecting people together.

When we started the exchange between children and the elderly, I soon realized that the children were not used to dealing with elderly people. One of the reasons for this is that few children live in households where three generations live together. The children weren't relaxed. They didn't shun the aged, but apparently were not eager to come into close contact with them. Later, their attitude began to change, and they took the elderly people's hands and walked with them to the Go board and handed them a stone. I had not instructed them to do this, it was a spontaneous act. The elderly must have felt that the children were adorable, and the exchange between them turned into a very warm one.

Recently, some facilities that combine services for the elderly with a nursery school have been designed. These are supposed to provide an opportunity for interaction between these two groups, but this often proves very difficult. Such exchange looks good on paper, but what can be done in practice, such as children singing songs for the elderly, is very limited. Unable to find many ways to interact, these facilities welcomed exchanges through Go when I visited them in Fukuoka. Through playing Capture Go, children are able to learn kindness from the elderly, and the elderly are able to regain some spirit from the children.

The exchanges have expanded slowly and Go games by mail have started between the day care centers for the elderly in Yuzamachi, Yamagata prefecture and Fukuoka prefecture. Playing Capture Go by mail is done by marking your next move on a paper board

An elderly player places a stone

and sending it to the opponent along with letters, drawings, and photographs.

After I made my first visit to Yuzamachi in October 1996, I visited there every two months. Capture Go is now played in all the nursery schools, kindergartens, elementary and junior high schools, as well as the homes for the elderly and mentally disabled in the town. It is wonderful that people who knew nothing about Go were impressed by the exchanges and are expanding them into other areas. All the groups have begun to have exchanges with each other, among them a prefectural school for the deaf in Sakata city.

A conversation with a nursery school child was the key to my visiting the school for the deaf. The child was a really good player, so I asked her if she played Capture Go at home. She replied that she teaches Go to her brother who attends the school for the deaf. I told her to continue, for it is a wonderful thing to do. After the conversation, I asked Mr. Sato to let me visit the school for the deaf. Mr. Sato agreed, since one of his friends is an office worker at the school and he felt that they would surely accept my offer.

Visiting the school, I talked about the reason I started my program and my experiences to the principal and the vice principal. The female vice principal listened to it in tears. And they asked me to teach Capture Go to their children.

41

First, I visited a class of junior high school students. On my way to the room, there was an elementary school child who stood in the corridor alone. The vice principal asked him why he was standing there, but only received a very ambiguous response. I told him to come with me since I was going to do something that was really fun.

There were seven junior high school students in all. Entering the room, I felt a bright atmosphere. Like ordinary schools, they soon started to play the capture game with enthusiasm. When the children's team played against the teachers' team, every child was very excited and cheered on the players. It created a wonderful atmosphere, which was somehow different from that at other schools. The children and the teachers had become one and I was fascinated by this. Then the elementary school children came into the room. I told the junior high school children to teach Go to these youngsters, now that they were good enough to do so.

The junior high school children started teaching them Capture Go immediately. You may imagine that the children use sign language, but the school discourages the use of sign language as much as possible because it hinders children's ability to read lips. Soon the elementary school children learned to play Go and we had an enjoyable competition.

On our returning to the principal's office, she talked about her school, which has three departments: nursery, elementary, and junior high. The teachers emphasize enriching the children's minds. They put their first priority on bringing the children into contact with various people and learning by themselves through enriching their minds, and have not put any priority on sign language or pronunciation skills. On hearing that, I understood why both the children and the teachers at the school are so nice, kind, and lively. I would like to popularize Go in all the schools for the deaf throughout Japan, and there should be exchanges between the deaf children and other school children. Something very wonderful will surely grow from this.

Voices from the Field

A statement from Mr. Daigo Hinata, a teacher at Sakata school for the deaf

Mr. Yasuda visited our school in March 1997. I was uncertain about this since I knew nothing about Go. However, the rule "surround to capture" was simple enough and our children were soon absorbed in playing Go.

There was a boy in my class whose face did not express any emotions. We began to play Go for five minutes each day to start the day. Eventually his face began to show expression on winning and losing. Until then he had never acted on his own initiative, but now he does so, and is able to express his emotions.

When teachers play Go with children, it is no longer a case of "teachers and children", but each of us playing it seriously and on the same footing. One of the virtues of Go is that you are conscious of the opponent in a natural way and communicate with each other without words.

We've put Go sets where our children gather, such as in corridors and at the entrance of the gymnasium, so that the children feel free to play Go during the breaks and after school. We have also had exchange meetings with the children from other schools and with the local people several times. The children of our school explained the rule and began playing Go. Through these exchanges, I have become convinced that the deaf children have learned how to interact with ordinary hearing people on the same footing. It will surely be a tool for developing good relationships with others and for gaining confidence when they are out in society in the future.

When playing, the children make quick judgments on the next move. They ask themselves what the best move is and decide it for themselves. It is a good experience for those who usually just imitate what others do and cannot take the initiative. I believe that the children will gain in confidence in other parts of their lives so that they can judge and act on their own.

At present, we are working on the principle "nurture the children to live strongly, and to overcome their hearing handicap". All the teachers have come to think of Go as one of the treasures that will enable the deaf children to live a full and satisfying life in the future.

Part Two: How to Create a Go Program

In my visits to schools and institutions nationwide many people have expressed an interest in introducing a Go program. I often receive invitations to visit as an instructor, but it is impossible to accept them all. If the rule "surround to capture" is understood, anyone can introduce the game.

Based on my personal experience, I have put together some important points on how to handle different groups and how to play the game with teams and with single players. I hope this will help you develop an efficient way to instruct beginners in Go.

Although more complex versions of Go with more difficult rules exist, here we apply only the simple rule "surround to capture" because we regard the game primarily as a means of improving interactions and communication. Some more complicated applications of this rule are discussed in the Appendix of the book. If you are confused by a situation in a game, check out these explanations, but don't worry about this. The most important thing is that, rather than trying to teach Go, you should try to create an opportunity to interact through playing Go. Go is especially effective as a means of interaction for children who are isolated and lack friends, or for those who are too sensitive to adults' feelings to come out of their shell.

On first taking up Go, there is no need to worry about the more difficult rules. On the contrary, if you introduce the more complex versions of the game in schools or mental institutions from the beginning, there is a high probability that you will fail to have a successful program. Teachers who have run Go programs emphasize this point. Being unfamiliar with Go has no bearing on the success of the program. Creating a fun atmosphere is paramount. If you can make children feel that Go is fun, this is tantamount to already succeeding in the program. In no time, children who rarely show emotion will have lively facial expressions. Go is a tool that anyone can use to make this happen.

In running a program, I take account of how young or old the beginners are, or how severe the mental disabilities are, and adjust the procedure accordingly, but the fundamentals in any situation remain the same as what I use for small children. The language ability of small children is underdeveloped, so they are unable to understand difficult explanations. It is therefore very important to create a fun atmosphere. If you can make small children like the game, you can surely do the same for elementary school children and the mentally disabled. Here, then, is how I proceed with a program for small children.

How to Teach Kindergarten Children

When teaching small children, creating a good atmosphere in the first minute is critical for success. Depending on whether the children's first impressions of me are friendly or cautionary, I change the way I start. For example, when small children are in a relaxed mood from the outset, things are sure to go smoothly. However, in most cases, small children are very cautious at first. It is natural for children to feel this way, since they are going to play Go for the first time in their life, and what's more, with a total stranger. It is very difficult to create a relaxed atmosphere if I talk only about Go. Therefore, I always start with an icebreaker to grab the children's interest.

I sometimes teach children as young as three, but I would like to focus on how I proceed with five year olds. When I begin a program at nursery schools or kindergartens, I ask to be given sixty minutes. An appropriate number of children is between twenty and thirty. You need a 9×9 demonstration Go board, such as the magnetic one seen in several pictures in this book. After introducing myself, I begin by saying, "Today I want to play a game with you." "Play" is one of the favorite words of children. I don't start talking about Go immediately, however. Instead, I ask some questions.

"Are you familiar with kanji characters?" I ask. Most children say that they are. I then write the character for "horse" or "fish" on the board and ask them what it is. The children usually give various answers, but if no one is willing to answer, I call on a particular child. When no one gives the correct answer, I give them a hint such as "It's an animal". Eventually, someone gives me the correct answer. I ask the child who gave the correct answer to come to the front and ask his or her name. Then I praise the child, saying, "Wow, you are great. Give (name) a big hand, everyone." Obviously, the child is very happy to be applauded. I then ask other questions such as what they think the horse is doing (running) and in which direction (to the left). Every time I get a correct answer, I ask for applause. In my opinion, applause is an important factor in creating a good atmosphere. Everyone clapping their hands creates a feeling of unity. I am always able to create a good atmosphere with this kind of quiz.

In creating a good atmosphere, it is very important that you also enjoy yourself. Children are so sensitive that if they feel a hint of unwillingness on your part, they will not feel any enthusiasm for the activity. Therefore I would like you to think of your own way to create a good atmosphere; in a nutshell, what is necessary to make the children laugh. You should do whatever you feel is right. If you are enjoying yourself, you will surely find that the children show an interest. Of course, when the children look happy from the beginning, you can start the games straight away without having the introductory activity. I usually spend about thirty or forty minutes on talking with the children, and after the children show happy expressions on their faces, I begin to talk about Go. You may think that this does not leave enough time for the games, but there is no need to worry. A game with teams can be fully enjoyed in only fifteen minutes.

The rules should be explained briefly: We use black and white playing pieces that are called stones, you place a stone where the lines intersect, and you surround a stone to capture it. Often children do not understand what "surround a stone to capture it" means. Since it is hard to make them understand with words alone, I ask if there is someone who can show us how to do it. I choose one of those who raise their hands and say, "You can use as many stones as you want,", and I let the child continue until he or she thinks it is right. You will often see a situation like Diagram 1. This is correct. Or you may see the pattern

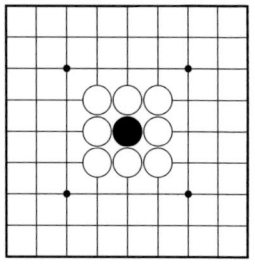

Diagram 1

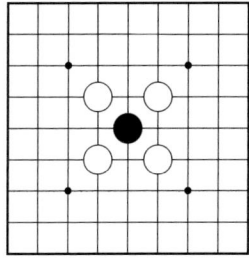
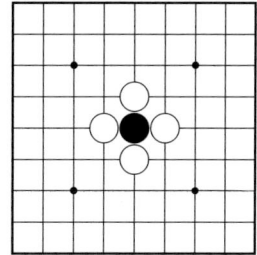

Diagram 2   *Diagram 3*

in Diagram 2, which is fine, also, as a case of surrounding. People who are familiar with Go would come up with the pattern Diagram 3 shows, and may feel uncomfortable with cases such as Diagrams 1 and 2. However, you should not expect the children to place stones as in Diagram 3 right away.

Once a child surrounds a stone, please give him or her a big hand. I repeat this a few times and tell them that a stone can be surrounded using only four stones, and ask if anyone can show us how to do it. After a child places stones as in Diagram 3, I explain that this is the best way to surround a stone to capture it. I ask the child who placed the stones correctly to remove the black stone. I then ask the other children to give him or her a big hand. Then I place the black stone back on the board and explain that the lines on the board are like streets and the four streets that extend from the black stone are dead ends now, since the white stones are blocking them. The black stone now has nowhere to escape, and is therefore captured. By this time, most of the children are able to understand what "surround to capture" means. Of course, there are some children who will not have understood yet. Nevertheless, you should begin playing the game.

To play a game, I put up a large demonstration Go board, and have the children form teams. A good number for a team is around ten. The members of each team take turns placing a stone. First, I ask the teachers to divide the children into teams. Then I ask them to stand in lines. The two children at the head of the lines play a game of rock, scissors, paper to decide which team goes first. Then the teams exchange greetings of *onegaishimasu* (see page 17) and the game begins, using the rule that the first team to make a capture wins. I call the first child forward and hand over a stone, making it a rule to hand a stone to each child individually. The first player uses the black stones and places the stone anywhere he or she likes, returning to the end of the line. The children cheer each other on, especially when stones are about to surround and capture other stones. When one of the teams surrounds a stone or a string of stones and captures it, the game is over. We give the child who made a capture a big hand. At the end of the game, the two teams face and thank each other for playing the game. When there is more time, I ask the children to play Go one on one, using a small board.

This is not a difficult process, of course, and most children enjoy the games. However, some do not take to it, perhaps due to hypersensitivity to adults, namely, the teachers and myself. Getting these children to play happily is one of our main objectives, so in the next section I will make several points about dealing with these children.

Most children are fascinated by Go, though I still wonder why this is so. Watching children play I have noticed that there is a moment when a child's look suddenly brightens. This is usually when they succeed in capturing stones by themselves. That is, they discover the move that captures by themselves, which leads to increased confidence. In fact, if an adult tells them where to play, it deprives the child of the joy of discovery, so I never tell a child where to play to make a capture.

Of course, some children can't find the right place to play and don't know what to do. In such cases, I give a hint such as, "Can you find some stones that you can capture around here?" or "You're close." However, I never say where to place the stone, and if they don't find the right place, I just leave it. Often during games there are many chances to capture stones, and eventually children will see their chance. It is important to be patient, even though the situation may be obvious to you.

I remember one case: A child's stones were chased to the edge of the board and were about to be captured. So to prevent this, the child played a stone beyond the edge of the grid. I was struck by how flexible children can be and thought, "How important is it for them to follow the usual rules?" This child's solution to a problem was amazing – though the child who discovered how to chase the stones to the edge was even more amazing. I saw no reason to stop them when they were enjoying their game. If one of them protests, they can think and find a way to deal with the situation. It's quite alright for them to create their own rule. I consider it one of the objects of playing Go that children express their opinions and find agreeable solutions on their own.

Patience is important, but it can be difficult. Often children are so concerned about how adults feel that they just stand in front of the board and don't play a stone. In such cases, I simply wait until the child acts on his or her own. Sometimes this can take five minutes, which can seem like a long time. But if you can hold out and not push the child, sometimes surprising things happen. The other children may be restless at first and ask the child to make a play, but often they begin to offer encouragement and cheer the child on. And when the child finally plays, they will spontaneously applaud, regardless of how good this move was. While waiting, I try to focus on the child and not let my mind wander. Children will notice when we lose interest, and this can cast a chill over the situation.

Children are fully aware of when they are the center of attention and receiving applause for an act can have a dramatic effect. It is not unusual for children who barely express emotion to suddenly light up.

Not all children will take to Go immediately. There are always some who are too shy to stand in front of others or who run around the room pretending indifference. I prefer to give these children free rein, though you will probably need to tell the teachers in advance not to try to force them to participate. The reason for this approach is that these children are the ones who will be changed the most by Go.

If this doesn't work, you can try playing a one on one game with these children, but it is not really a problem. Not all children are alike. If some don't join in, there is no reason to criticize them. From my experience, I think it is better to let children take their own course.

When introducing Go to a group, I begin with team competition, but if time permits, I introduce one on one games as well. The rule can be the same as in the team games, that is, the first to capture anything wins, but in one on one games you can also say that in order to win you must capture at least three stones, or five, etc. The two players use a game of rock, scissors, paper to decide who goes first. One on one play is usually very quiet as the players concentrate fully on the game and seem to be in heart to heart communication. So, while team games build up group spirit and create a happy atmosphere, one on one games seem to deepen communication and allow a warm atmosphere to fill everyone's heart.

Children playing at a demonstration board

Children who are initially friendless begin to make more friends and gain more confidence after enjoying several one on one games. Children who previously performed mischievous things to get the teacher's attention will become calmer by playing one on one games with the teacher. Children who wouldn't listen to others will become able to listen carefully, and children who couldn't express themselves will become able to express opinions. This is really the result of the inborn abilities of children; Go is just the trigger to bring it out. Communication on a deeper level can solve many problems spontaneously, and Go is the most effective tool for this that I have been able to discover.

The most successful programs make Go sets available for the children to play as they wish. When children have free time, they can play as much as they like. This relaxed attitude is key. If there is a set time for Go, this can become an added burden on the teacher. Go should simply be an activity that is available as a part of informal activities.

In playing Go it is very important for both sides to face each other squarely. I encourage teachers to play with children who request it, but it is not necessary to sit in a small chair to get down to the child's level. What matters is the attitude toward the child. As long as adults focus on the child and try to seriously interact with them, it will be fine. The child needs to feel the teacher's attention.

Even if the teacher can only find a few minutes to play with the children, it is important to do so. This provides a way to interact with the children, and it also helps the children to grow confident about relating to other people. I've seen this happen many times. Go is a tool for interpersonal interaction.

How to Teach Elementary School Children

Introducing Go and creating a good atmosphere is a little easier with students older than five. It also becomes possible to have Go activities involving the entire student body. Gathering several hundred students into the gymnasium I introduce the game in the usual way and choose two teams for a demonstration game. Then I have all the students play a practice one on one game with someone sitting next to them, having distributed small boards to everyone. After that, we randomly choose teams from each grade and one team of teachers. These teams play a tournament on the large demonstration board at the front and it is very exciting. Often the younger students will win, and it is quite rare for the teachers' team to triumph. This kind of interaction with the teachers is very good for students – especially when the teachers lose! I recommend having this sort of tournament a couple of times a year.

You do not need to be a good Go player to be a good teacher of Go in this sort of program. In fact it is an advantage for the teacher to be on the same level as the children, given the goals of the program. Even if the teacher does not know the game well, he or she can still encourage the children and cheer them on.

Sometimes very complicated patterns of stones will develop in a game, and you may not notice that some stones have in fact been surrounded. This is not a problem. I recommend that you have a rule that the first player who realizes that the stones are surrounded wins the game. Everyone seems to find this special rule quite reasonable.

It is obviously good for students to interact with teachers on an even basis. Moreover, children can learn important things from seeing how the teachers deal with the struggle to get better and the experiences of winning and losing.

When dealing with several classes at once, I encourage individual teachers to come up and play one on one games. It is good for the students to see their teachers playing each other, and they will cheer the teachers on, even if the teacher was not particularly popular before the game. Children don't want their teacher to lose.

This is good for both parties. Teachers are usually not accustomed to being cheered by their students, so this can be a very energizing experience. And children can develop a more positive attitude toward a teacher after such a game. I feel this activity is particularly important for teachers who think they lack a good relationship with their students.

How to Teach Junior High and High School Students

Older students are usually apathetic, or perhaps they're just tired. They sometimes have a apparent distrust of adults. Compared to younger children, you need more effort to attract their attention. Therefore, I always begin by talking about relationships with the opposite sex. Given the probable expectations the students have for a lecture on Go, raising this topic always changes the atmosphere. I ask those who are dating someone to raise their hands, and some do, while others are too shy to do so. When the atmosphere has relaxed, I introduce the game in the usual way and start off with boy-girl pair teams, which works well with this age group. After the demonstration game, I have the group play practice games one on one, and then have the same sort of tournament I hold in elementary schools. I conclude with a tournament between teams of teachers, because cheered by the students is a good tonic for them. I always emphasize connecting the teachers and students through Go.

How to Teach Go in Institutions

Go programs have been introduced into schools for the deaf, schools for handicapped children, homes for the mentally disabled, and homes for the elderly. Running a Go program in such institutions is not difficult, but your proposal may meet with initial resistance because of the preconception that Go is a difficult game. It is true that some disabled people are never able to understand the concept of "surround to capture", but in an extreme case you can just stand around a board and place stones. Being applauded for any action can be a positive experience for many people in such situations.

With a disabled group I follow the usual approach, finding a way to get someone to come up and place a stone. Sometimes I have to help the person to do this, but I always ask for a big hand when the stone gets placed on an intersection, even if it's not on an intersection. This changes the atmosphere completely, and things usually go smoothly after that. Of course, the pace is much slower than in school.

People in institutions tend to rarely have an opportunity for being recognized by others for doing something. Getting recognition with loud applause for the first time can help them develop more confidence.

When it's possible, I explain the "surround to capture" rule in these situations, though some people never get it. Some will always place the stone in a square, but it doesn't matter. I slide it to an intersection and ask for the person to be applauded.

Time moves slowly in these homes, but the people enjoy the time spent playing Go. You can easily see this in their changed facial expressions and in comments about looking forward to playing. Few of them play on their own, but even playing only on my bimonthly visits can change their lives. Sometimes the changes are dramatic with people becoming much more animated and even more physically agile. This is wonderful. It would be an interesting subject for research.

Voices from the Field

A statement from Mrs. Rie Baba, a teacher at Sunayama nursery school in Fukuoka

Sunayama nursery school is a multiple use facility that also houses a day care center for the elderly and an after school club for elementary school children. In February 1996, we began Go activities for our children because we agree with what Mr. Yasuda is trying to achieve. Now the nursery school children, the elderly at the day care center and the elementary school children in the after school club all enjoy playing Go every day. A lively atmosphere is created as the children chase the elderly to get them to play Go together.

We put emphasis on "interaction" at our school. When we play Go, quality communication can take place because we face each other as we play. The children appear to have changed through playing Go. For example, a boy who was not good at interacting with others has now become a good Go player and gets along with others more confidently. The boy asked to have a Go set as his birthday present from his parents. Although he cannot read yet, he looks forward to finding the Go section in the newspaper. His parents were impressed by this change.

We think it is very important for fathers to take an interest in the education of their children, but it has been very difficult to get them involved. However, this boy's father has become the chairman of the Father's Association and enthusiastically asks other fathers to participate in their children's education. I believe that this is one of the great benefits of the Go program.

Another benefit of the Go program is that through playing Go with the elderly at the day care center, the children have developed kindness and consideration for others. Each child seems to be more independent and more confident than before.

Part Three: The Program Expands Around the World

The First Go Program Overseas – in the Netherlands

My efforts to bring people together through Go have now expanded outside Japan. My horizons were broadened by an incident at Nokonoshima in Fukuoka prefecture. Exchange between the Himawari-no-sato home and Nokonoshima nursery school had grown, and people throughout the island had come to enjoy Capture Go. At a graduation ceremony at Nokonoshima nursery school, where there is a tradition that each child talks about his or her dreams, one of the girls talked about her dream to become a Go teacher. Imagining the girl wanted to become a Go professional, her father asked her why she had this dream. "In want to popularize Go throughout the world," she replied, "and play Go with everyone in friendship."

The girl's father was surprised by this, but I myself was even more so when I heard about it later. When someone talks of becoming a teacher of Go, they usually refer to becoming a Go professional. However, this girl did not mean that she wanted to study Go and enjoy it for herself, but rather that she wanted people throughout the world to live in harmony through playing Go. From then on, I began to think about promoting my Go program outside of Japan.

Soon after that, I was informed that an important Go title match was to be held in the Netherlands. The Netherlands is the home of Mr. Frank Janssen, who had visited me in Japan and was enthusiastic about my Capture Go program. On that occasion we had visited Omachi city in Nagano prefecture and taught Go to the children in a hospital. Mr. Janssen well understood that Go could be utilized not just as a hobby, but also in the fields of education, social work, and therapy, and he had actually started a Capture Go program in the Netherlands. Not wanting to miss the chance to help popularize Go outside of Japan, I asked the Yomiuri Newspaper Company, the sponsor of the title match, to send me to the Netherlands, and they agreed to do so.

This was January 1996, and it was my first opportunity to try my program abroad. Since I don't speak English, let alone Dutch, I was uncertain whether the language problem might hinder the Go program from proceeding smoothly. I also didn't know whether or not children in the Netherlands would like Go. I was convinced that children in any country should be able to enjoy Go, but I was not sure if I could create a good enough atmosphere through an interpreter to make them enthusiastic about playing.

To create a good atmosphere, I played "rock, scissors, paper" and sang Japanese songs. I also wrote down the kanji character for "horse" and gave them a quiz as to the meaning of it. These activities all helped to break the ice.

I then introduced the principle of "surround to capture" and soon the children started playing some games. The children were at least as excited as Japanese children. Soccer is very popular in the Netherlands and the excitement was similar to that of fans at a soccer match. They stamped on the floor, shouted, and created a great commotion. The teachers were amazed that a Japanese could suddenly visit the school from the other side of the world and cause such a big sensation.

The schools I visited were a private Jewish school and a Montessori school. The children at both schools were excited about playing Go, but the visit to the Montessori school was particularly impressive. There is no set curriculum at the school: each child has his or her chosen tasks each day, and the teachers help them if necessary. Of course, the children are not allowed a completely free reign, and if a child bothers other children, the teachers are quite strict in disciplining him. It seemed that the teachers there aim at a balance between instructing the children and yet at the same time letting them discover things for themselves. When I started the Go program at the school, the teachers started gathering in the classroom in ones and twos and by the end they were all absorbed in games. They told me later that Go fits in well with the Montessori methods and they showed a strong interest in it.

The atmosphere of schools varies from country to country, though maybe it is more appropriate to say that the character of the teachers varies. For example, I saw the teachers playing with the children during the break in the Netherlands. Also, I often saw that a teacher stayed with a child while studying, on a one to one basis. In Japan, I don't see teachers playing with children very often. In some cases, there were even teachers who started doing their own chores while I played Go with the children. Are the teachers in Japan too busy? I have visited six countries in Europe and realized that the children in each country find their teachers "cool". The teachers attract the children. At the same time, the children's response to Go appeared to be exactly the same as I had observed with Japanese children.

I visited the Netherlands on two later occasions, and over a period of time the perception of Go has changed among the people involved, including Mr. Janssen. An organization has been set up in the Netherlands called The European Go Cultural Center where they strive to popularize Go throughout Europe. Mr. Janssen works for the organization, and all the people in the organization including the man in charge, Mr. Eric Puyt, have thought deeply about the beneficial aspects of Capture Go. Through the internet they have started to tell people in other countries about Go activities at schools and introduce the teachers and children who are playing Go in the Netherlands. Go has such a great power.

– in Romania

When I was visiting schools in the Netherlands, I encountered a young man from Romania, a Mr. Roberto Mateescu. While he was student, he came to Japan to study Go, and he was a fellow pupil of my own Go teacher. Moved by the program at the school, he asked me to visit Romania, and eight months later, I was able to visit him there.

I visited several schools in Romania, and as I said before, I found the atmosphere of schools differs from country to country. In Romania, after the collapse of the Soviet Union, the economy was not in good shape. Romania is an agricultural country, so they have plenty of food, but little else. Compared to Japan, practically nothing was available. On the other hand, I felt great warmth from their hearts, from every person I met. On our way from Bucharest to Braila, we dropped in at the house of Roberto's grandmother. As soon as his grandmother came out from the house, she hugged me and put her cheek against my cheek. I'll never forget the warmth of it.

When we arrived in Braila, we visited a school. There was a teacher called Miss Liliana Iacob who had founded a Go club and enjoyed playing with the children. She had established the Go club simply because Go was an interesting game. She had no particular intention to educate or to aid communication.

The school was similar to a Japanese elementary school and junior high school combined, and the children's ages varied from seven to fifteen. I asked her to gather together the children who weren't familiar with Go. I was taken to what looked like a science room, partially sunk below ground level, where there were about one hundred children waiting for me.

We began playing, and soon the children were creating quite a commotion. When I looked out of the windows, I realized that there were many children who were peering into the room where we were playing. Their eyes were full of curiosity, wanting to know what we were doing.

There were some teachers observing the games who seemed to take an interest. They asked me to teach Go to their classes, also, so I visited the same school the following day. This time I visited the three classes for seven year olds. They were so adorable, and their eyes had a different sparkle to them: They appeared to gaze up at me with a passion for learning. I wonder whether that is the true nature of children?

Japanese children's eyes also sparkle when playing Go, but the children in Romania were different somehow. They took an interest in everything and were eager to learn anything. I imagine that if Japanese children could have an exchange visit with these wonderful children in Romania, they would come more alive.

The children in the school in Romania loved Go so much that it became the talk of the school and more than three hundred children stormed into Miss Iacob's Go club. She had to ask for help. She asked Mr. Iulian Toma, who runs a hospital in Braila and is chairman of the Romanian Go Association, to help her. Mr. Toma was a good player and was willing to offer help, but this later created problems. Mr. Toma had not seen how the Go program was done when I visited the school, and the intentions of the Go program were not conveyed to him properly.

Two years later, in 1998, I had a chance to visit Braila again and met Mr. Toma. He began to talk about the Go club. "Do you know what happened to the Go club?" he asked. I anticipated what was coming and said, "Maybe the number of club members has fallen to fifty or something?" He replied, "Actually, it has fallen to five!" I asked what he did at the Go club. It turned out that Mr. Toma had explained the tactics that Japanese Go professionals use and talked about very difficult things. He had tried to make the children better players and had thus taught them Go tactics very strictly. No wonder the children had walked away!

I had Mr. Toma watch me play Capture Go with the children and explained why I have continued the program. I myself had had a bitter experience when I tried to teach the more difficult rules. I had given about five hundred children Go-phobia. So I said to Mr. Toma, "You are allowed to put up five hundred people off Go; you are not to be criticized." His reply was, "I've nearly reached my limit already!" We both burst out laughing. By this time he fully understood what I was doing with the program, so I doubt he will repeat the same mistake.

On my second trip to Braila we used a cultural center in the town for the program and there were more than one hundred children from several schools. The children really enjoyed playing Go. One of the teachers who participated in the games was so impressed that I was invited to his school the following day. The room again looked like a science room, and about a hundred and fifty children were packed in like sardines, waiting for me. There was supposed to be only one class for the program, but the teacher had talked about the program to other teachers, and they also wanted to join in. So there were four or five classes all together, but I noticed that the children who played Go at the cultural center were not in the room. Those children joined us later in the middle of the program. I wondered why and later asked the reason. It turned out that one of the children who had played Go at the cultural center had asked the teacher why they couldn't join the Go program that day. The teacher told them that they had had games on the previous day and now it was the other children's turn to play. One of the children started crying and asked the teacher to let them join the program, saying, "We want to hear more of the Go teacher's talk." The teacher was so moved by the remark that he decided to let them join half way through.

I heard that story when I was having dinner with the people involved. They said that the children wanted to hear me talk more, but I had not talked about anything special. Besides, the children heard my story through an interpreter and I was not sure how well the children understood me. What had happened was that we were able to communicate from heart to heart, and I believe that Go greatly contributed to that.

– in the Czech Republic

We tend to see Europe as one entity, but the atmosphere in Western European countries such as the Netherlands, Belgium, and France is quite different from that in Eastern European countries such as Romania and the Czech Republic. Of course, the state of the economy in Eastern Europe is also quite different, but I got the impression that the people are guileless. In September 1998, I visited the Czech Republic for the first time and played Go with about one thousand children. I have particularly vivid memories of a teacher training college in the Czech Republic. When I played Go with thirty sixteen year old students, they treated me with great hospitality. The school is in a town called Liberec. Some of the students dressed in their traditional costumes and treated me to bread and beer, which is the customary way to greet guests.

I sang some songs and talked about some kanji characters as I always do. Soon, the students were relaxed and it was time to play Go. I first asked them to divide into a black team and a white team but they replied, "We already have!" Then I realized that all the students were dressed either in black or in white. That was one on me! After we played the games, we had an informal discussion.

"It might be beyond your comprehension, but in Japan,

children of your age are killing themselves," I told them. They looked puzzled. They didn't understand the situation because they thought that life around that age should be full of fun. "We can buy anything with money in Japan. We can do anything. Food and clothes are abundant. However, when people lose heart, they can become dangerous weapons," I continued. I then talked about the controversial problem of bullying. "The children in a group start to bully one child. Other children who witness the bullying will not help the bullied child so as not to become victims themselves. At worst, they join the offenders. It is very sad that some children become isolated and commit suicide." I realized that on hearing the story, one of the boys was crying. The children in the Czech Republic and the children in Japan live on the same planet and are the same innocent children. Why then, depending on where children live, can the situation differ to such a degree?

I had brought paper Go boards from Japan and I handed one to each child. After the talk, a young teacher in his twenties approached me. The teacher was also shedding tears. The teacher asked me to autograph the back of the paper Go board. Watching that, all the students crowded around me, asking for my autograph. I said, half in jest, "I'll give you my autograph if you kiss me on the cheek."

The students at the school seemed to have both feet firmly on the ground. Compared to Japanese high school students, they appeared very mature. The students in the Czech Republic were able to understand why I've been trying to expand Go and that all people are equal. After graduating from the school, each student will work as a teacher, and they promised me that they would convey the virtue of Go to many people.

– in Poland

I visited a town called Wodzislaw in Poland near the border with the Czech Republic where a Mr. Jan Lubos, a good Go player, lives. He is such a good player that he has participated in the World Amateur Go Championship, and while in Japan, Mr. Lubos had visited some kindergartens and homes for the disabled with me and understood my aims. I had not planned to visit Poland, but Mr. Lubos wanted me to visit there at any cost so we decided to go there in spite of our tight schedule. I was invited to two schools.

Despite being in the countryside of Eastern Europe, not everything was calm and simple. At one of the schools in particular, I visited a class of fourteen and fifteen year olds where the teachers' expressions indicated that the students were out of control. When I entered the room, they were very noisy and defiant.

I had prior warning of the situation at the school from Mr. Lubos. He told me that as Poland made the shift from a communist to a capitalist economy the country had put the highest priority on striving to rebuild the economy. As a result the country put less priority on education and this has caused various social problems. Mr. Lubos worried whether I would be able to have a Go lesson because the children were unable to concentrate on one thing. However, I felt that this was precisely where Go should be helpful. Ignoring the situation in the classroom, I began a game of Go as always. Soon we had games between the teachers and the children, which got them excited. The children were frustrated over losses and overjoyed by wins, hugging each other tight. It was such a wonderful time.

At the other school, we ran the program after school, and attendance was open to anyone. I expected only ten or twenty would come, but about one hundred children turned up. There was a game between eight year olds and fifteen year olds. The teachers' team joined the games later and their games added to the fun. The principal of the school was a wonderful lady of around forty. She was moved by the experience and told me that she will incorporate Go into their lessons. I was invited to the principal's office and treated to a meal along with wine, brandy, and champagne. When I asked her if her office was often used for this kind of party, she told me that it was the first time in school history that such a party had been held in the principal's office! I believe they continue to have a Go lesson once a week for second graders and above, and once every two weeks for first graders.

– in Hungary

In Europe I visited several schools, but I also visited an institute for the disabled in Budapest, Hungary. Children who suffer from cerebral palsy are hospitalized in the institute for rehabilitation. The facility, called PETO, is very big, similar to one at a university hospital in Japan. The children come not only from Hungary, but also from all around the world. Peto is the name of the person who invented their rehabilitation method. PETO has been using various methods for rehabilitation and I had high expectations that Go could be a great help in their program.

I was first invited into a room where the Hungarian children were gathered. The teachers in the room looked bewildered, not knowing what was going to happen. The children showed little expression. I sang an action song called, "Open, close them," in Japanese, which I often sing at schools. The children tried their best to imitate me by moving their hands. Then I talked about the kanji character for "horse", and the children's expressions began to change.

We started to play Go and it was unbelievable to see how the children were smiling. Some of the children whose bodies were so stiff that they could not stretch their arms nor open their palms tried hard to place a stone on the Go board. The teachers were completely surprised by this and said that they would like to incorporate Go as one of their rehabilitation routines.

Then I visited the international ward and played Go with children from various countries. These children also played Go happily. The teacher said to me later, "Japan is such a wonderful country! It's splendid that you have incorporated Go into your education system." The teachers at PETO took me to be a teacher from Japan and thought I was there to introduce them to the wonderful Japanese education system. I didn't know how to reply!

What moved the teachers at PETO especially was that the children's expressions brightened. That a foreigner like me could visit them, and simply by playing Go, could reap such wonderful smiles from the children seemed beyond comprehension. However, I now firmly believe that their smiles were nothing special, but are something that all children naturally possess. Is it just that as adults, teachers, and parents, we tend to put labels on children and the disabled, and therefore cannot see them as they truly are? Go acts as a catalyst and we are given a glimpse of our true selves. Children always smile when they are enjoying themselves.

Hungary emphasizes education for small children. In the city of Keszthely there is a school for kindergarten and elementary school children that has strong ties with Japan; in fact it was founded with donations from Japan. The school is named Japan-Hungary Friendship Tree School and looks very different from schools in Japan. For example, all the play equipment in the school's grounds is made of wood, and it is obvious that every effort is made to help the children develop free ideas. Until then, I hadn't seen any difference between kindergartens in Japan and those in other countries, but this kindergarten in Hungary was different.

The principal of the kindergarten has a dream to make the kindergarten the best in the world, and she talked to one of her Japanese acquaintances about including Go in the educational program. I heard about this and decided to visit the school. I played Go with every class, from three to nine year olds. The principal watched the children's lively expressions and told me that she wanted to include Go as part of the curriculum, not just as another game.

– in the USA

Dr. William Cobb, from Virginia, has been actively working on a Go program. While teaching philosophy at university, he tries to popularize Go in the USA. When Dr. Cobb visited Japan, in February and March 1998, we had the opportunity to visit schools together. On returning to the USA, Dr. Cobb started visiting schools to teach Go. He thought that the simple capturing game would be helpful in popularizing Go among children. Capturing a stone by yourself is a shared delight anywhere in the world. Dr. Cobb has been popularizing Go to hundreds of children a year, and what has surprised him is that he witnessed the same phenomenon in the USA he had observed in Japan.

There are various problems in schools in the USA, too, particularly as a result of its being a multi-cultural society which sometimes causes a breakdown in communication. Development in controlling emotions may be stymied as a result. Dr. Cobb told me that such children often become calm after starting to play Go and are better able to get along with others. Their academic achievement has also improved.

Among the schools visited by Dr. Cobb was Thompson Middle School in Richmond, Virginia, where over ninety percent of the students are African American. This school did a study of the impact of learning Go on its students. In 1997, two sixth grade classes played Go once a week for the entire year. The school decided to do a study, comparing these classes to others that did not play Go. They considered seven points, including ability to solve a problem on their own, scientific ways of thinking, improvements in math, and interaction with others. The children in the Go classes scored consistently higher than others, especially with regard to ability to solve a problem on their own, which had been a weak point before. Other schools reported similar effects. While these reports focused on academic improvement, Dr. Cobb pointed out that there were other kinds of improvement also.

The very first group to whom Dr. Cobb taught Go in a school was a group of fourteen year olds who had behavioral problems and who often didn't show up for school. He didn't know their reputation when he started teaching them, and he wasn't surprised when they were always present and sat quietly through the sessions, concentrating on their playing, but the school staff noticed. The principal came to the class just to see what had caused such a transformation in the students. He has also had parents come to visit his classes because they want to see what it is that is having such a big impact on their children.

In general, the students who learned to play Go do better on tests afterwards and also benefit from better social and emotional skills. There are now many schools in the USA with Capture Go programs.

Voices from the Field

A comment from Mr. Takashi Hayashi, founder of the Children's Go Association in Hatsukaichi, Hiroshima

I had long believed that we could make good use of Go in order to foster healthy and strong minds in children. After retirement, I tried to explain the virtues of Go to people around me, but they wouldn't listen. Then, I happened to read an article about Mr. Yasuda in a newspaper. I felt as if I had finally found a way to utilize Go. I accompanied Mr. Yasuda to observe the Go program that was held at a preschool and an institution for physically disabled people in Fukuoka in December 1998. I asked Mr. Yasuda to visit Hatsukaichi to introduce the Go program. However, Mr. Yasuda replied that "You can do it, Mr. Hayashi. It's a good challenge for you."

I had no choice but to try out the Go program by myself. After I returned to Hatsukaichi, I visited a nursery school near my house and talked of the purpose of the Go program to the principal. Fortunately, she agreed to my proposal. With Go sets that I bought from the Nihon Ki-in, I emulated Mr. Yasuda's activity. In no time, I realized that there was nothing to worry about. The children were very happy to play Go. Since then, I have expanded the Go activities to four nursery schools, a kindergarten, club activities at elementary schools and a day care center for elderly people.

I didn't have any real difficulty introducing Go, since the rules are quite simple, but I was once at a loss how to deal with a child when he burst out crying on losing a game. I told the child that he would be a better player because of the losses and he stopped crying.

As soon as I began the Go program, I experienced moving results. There are two children who were mildly autistic at one of the nursery schools and they used to spend the day just sitting in the corner of the playground. The principal told me that they have started to associate with others after the Go program was incorporated into the school's activities. Looking at the principal's surprised face, I myself was surprised since I had not been able to tell that the children were autistic.

My activities were introduced in an article in the city news bulletin, and I now have many people who offer cooperation. Since the number of the institutions we visit increased, it was impossible to deal with that many on my own. Therefore I've set up a Children's Go Association with my friends and now each person is in charge of a certain school or institution. Nowadays, many organizations hope to incorporate the Go program. I'd like to join hands with my friends to expand the circle of Go activity further.

A Common Wish

There is one thing that I noticed while meeting both adults and children in various countries. Everyone, adults and children, even those with "problems", have the same wish for peace and happiness. Even when we were not able to communicate verbally, their wishes were conveyed to me. Watching the sparkling in the children's eyes, I firmly believe that they are the true treasures of our planet. The sparkling in the children's eyes makes people around them happy. We must not let them lose that sparkle at any cost.

To date, people from more than twenty countries have visited Japan to learn about the Go program. Those people who liked it have begun the Go program in their own countries, and I would like to expand this network.

Epilogue

Nowadays in Japan we frequently hear of a "breakdown" in classes. I was shocked to hear that uncontrollable classes are occurring not only in senior and junior high schools, but even in elementary schools. From my experience, however, I feel somewhat uncomfortable with the expression "breakdown" being used to describe the situation at elementary schools.

On one occasion, I was playing Go with two combined first grade classes at an elementary school in Kumamoto prefecture. One of the classes was a so-called "uncontrollable" class. When the classroom teachers and I entered the room, one boy was lying on the floor. He ignored our entrance into the room and looked sulky. I asked the children whether they liked their school. All the children from one class raised their hands, while none of the other class moved an arm. Then I asked if they liked their teachers. Again, all the children of one class raised their hands, but the children of the other class did not. This was not unexpected. I have held Go activities in more than one thousand classes at elementary schools. I am now able to tell how well children are handled by just entering the classroom. I have observed that one class in three is in the so-called uncontrollable state. Uncontrollable sounds dramatic, but I don't think we should make to much of it. It is, simply put, the fact that a good relationship between the teacher and the children has not developed. I do not think we can blame it on either the teacher or the children.

"I'm here today to play a fun game called Go," I began. The children cheered up on hearing this and their eyes lit up, but the boy who lay on the floor said that he didn't want to play. I do not force children to play, leaving them to act as they will. I therefore left the boy lying on the floor.

When I talk about this to teachers, they tend to think that what I am doing is ignoring the child, but this is not the case. It may look as if I am ignoring these children, but actually I am giving them my full attention. I believe this produces unexpected developments. Teachers often claim to have witnessed "miracles" on these occasions, but I believe anyone can create such miracles if they truly concentrate with their whole being.

I quizzed the children on the kanji character for "horse" and talked of various things, which eventually relaxed them. Then we started playing Capture Go. Watching the other children's growing excitement, I noticed the boy who had been lying on the floor sneak into the line to play Go.

After the children played Go for a while, I had the teachers of the two classes play against each other. Both were women teachers, but they presented a study in contrast. The one who was popular among the students looked very cheerful and wore a big smile, while the other teacher looked pale and anxious. The cheers form the children also differed greatly. The children of the popular teacher cheered her on at the top of their lungs, but the other class did not utter a sound.

Hearing the children cheering on their teacher, the children of the other class looked unhappy. Even though they didn't have a good relationship with their teacher, it was vexing that their teacher was losing the game. Soon, one of the children started cheering on the unpopular teacher. The other children followed. By the end of the game, the children of both classes were cheering their teachers on. The teacher who had looked pale and serious now looked bewildered. She had never expected her children to cheer her on. Her complexion brightened and she concentrated on the game. Soon, the teacher of the uncontrollable class had a chance to capture some stones. Surprisingly, it was the boy who had been lying on the floor who shouted, "You can win! I'll show you where to place your stone!" and dashed to the teacher. "Here! Put a stone down here and you can win!" The teacher now realized where to place her stone and proceeded to capture her opponent's stones. Shouts of joy went up from the children.

I visited the teacher's class again some time later and realized that the atmosphere had completely changed. The boy who had been lying on the floor now sat at his desk properly so that I had to search to find him. That day we again enjoyed playing Capture Go. At the end of the games, all the children sat upright on the floor and thanked me for the games in a decorous manner. The teacher came to me and said, "The boy has changed, hasn't he?" It was true all right, but more than anything the teacher herself had changed. Her expression bore little resemblance to my previous visit; she looked very beautiful and full of confidence. I wondered if she had noticed the change in herself.

The Go program circles have expanded from the kindergarten in Shonai, Fukuoka, to various places in Japan. Among them is a town called Takamori in Kumamoto prefecture, where all the children under the age of twelve have learned to play Capture Go. A Children's Go Festival, sponsored by the Kumamoto Prefectural Board of Education, saw the introduction of Capture Go to the town. Once the venue for the Children's Go Festival had been decided, Mr. Toshiaki Kurihara, my partner in devising the plan, and I visited the town council to introduce ourselves. Mr. Kurihara is a former policeman who now has Go classes in Kumamoto city. What he offers at the class is more than just teaching Go, he also helps children in their development. Mr. Kurihara says watching children grow up is what he lives for.

The town board of education was ordered to have the Children's Go Festival by the prefectural board of education. The people in charge felt some exasperation: "We are very busy this time of the year," they explained. However, they had no choice but to accept the plan since it was an order from the top. What Mr. Kurihara and I had in mind was to enliven Takamori and the people through Go, and we tried hard to explain our plan. On our way from the town office, I told Mr. Kurihara that it might be impossible to make the people in this town understand the object of the Go program.

Next day, we visited a nursery school and an elementary school and played Capture Go for the first time there. The town official who accompanied us was responsible for the program. Less than one month later, that person called me and said, "We have decided to use Go as a means of helping in our young people's development. The town council has approved a budget for a Go program. Could you send Go sets to Takamori?"

I was reminded of the words Saigo Takamori, a politician who lived from 1822 to 1877, at the end of the Tokugawa Shogunate and the time of the Meiji Restoration. He said, "respect heaven and love the people." Everyone has a hope of his or her own.

I really believe that we should trust each other and be open to new things. Looking back on past experiences, everyone involved looked displeased at first. Despite that, I continued the program because I wanted to see children smile. Perhaps this desire in itself helped to change the expressions on the faces of the children and the disabled. It is also worth mentioning that the people who expressed the most apparent dislike on their faces were the ones who changed the most. If you give up hope upon receiving a bad response, you won't be able to achieve anything. Keeping in mind Saigo Takamori's words, "Respect heaven and love the people", I enjoyed playing Capture Go with the children in Takamori.

We Are All Alike Human Beings

There is an inn called Matisse where I always stay in Takamori. The owner of the inn is a wonderful person and every time I stay there, we enjoy conversing till late at night. One day the owner and I were enjoying a conversation with the person from the board of education who was in charge of the Children's Go Festival. The latter person had been working very hard for the sake of the town and its children. But he complained that no matter how hard he tried, the administration would not take the action he hoped for. The owner of the inn said, "You don't have to make everything into such a trial. Mr. Yasuda has visited Takamori simply to convey that we are all alike human beings."

My eyes were suddenly opened. "We are all alike human beings." I knew that I had had something like this in mind, but had not found the right words to explain it. The owner of the inn had expressed my very thoughts. I haven't had a higher education, and I've never studied subjects such as welfare or psychology. If I had done so, I probably wouldn't have realized that we are all alike human beings. I might, rather, have dealt with people full of my own prejudices, such as believing the disabled or small children have limited potential. I might also have overlooked the sparkle in children's eyes.

Appendix: More Detail on Capture Go

The basic rule of Capture Go is "surround to capture". Of course, this is not confined to a single stone; many stones that are connected as one group can be captured. During a game some patterns can arise that may cause perplexity. Some explanations are given below.

1. Surrounding a stone on the edge or in a corner

Stones in the center of the board must be surrounded from all four directions, but fewer stones are needed to surround on the edges or in the corners. In Diagram 1, the two black stones are both fully surrounded and captured. They should be removed from the board.

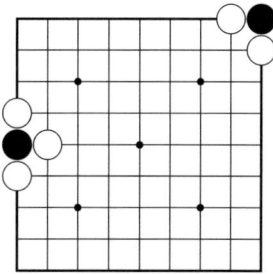

Diagram 1

2. Capturing a group

When several stones are connected horizontally and/or vertically, they form a group and can be captured as a whole. The three black groups in Diagram 2 have all been captured.

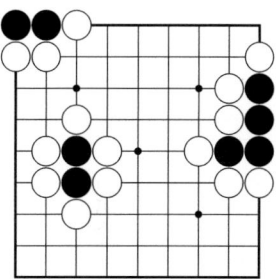

Diagram 2

3. Self-capturing by playing on an already surrounded point

In Diagram 3, if the four white stones are already in place and Black plays 1, Black 1 is immediately captured because it is already surrounded when it is played. This self-capturing play has the same effect as White playing so as to capture a black stone.

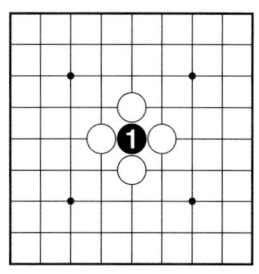

Diagram 3

4. When playing on an already surrounded point is not self-capture

What may look like a self-capturing move will not be if the play actually captures some stones of the other color. In Diagram 4, Black 1 captures the marked white stones, which are immediately removed, so Black 1 is not actually a self-capture. After Black 1 in Diagram 4, the board will appear as in Diagram 5.

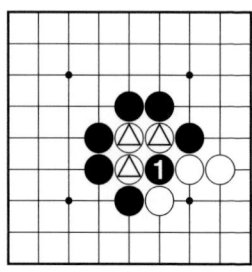

Diagram 4

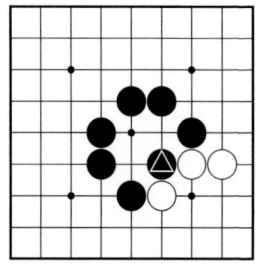

Diagram 5

5. A pattern in which Black and White can continually recapture each other's stone

The pattern in Diagram 6 is not uncommon. If Black plays 1 in Diagram 7, it captures the marked white stone, which is removed. If this does not end the game (because you are playing that it takes three captured stones to win, example), then White could capture the marked black stone as in Diagram 8. Then Black could recapture. This can continue until the number of stones needed to win have be captured. There is a special rule that applies to this situation in regular Go, but that is not necessary in the capture version of Go.

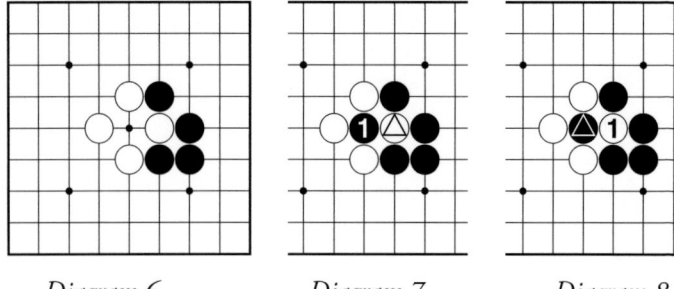

Diagram 6 *Diagram 7* *Diagram 8*

Afterword

As a journalist, I have reported on Mr. Yasuda's interactive Go program since its inception. Generally, Go is regarded as a difficult game, at which one either wins or loses. However, Mr. Yasuda's activities have challenged this view. Seeing this unfold was an amazing experience for me.

Helping with the writing of this book was a challenge for me. I wanted it to be Mr. Yasuda's expression of his own views and feelings, and yet the book needed to be an objective report on his activities as well. This was my first attempt at such a project. Drawing on my coverage of his activities for the past seven years, as well as the reactions of others, I believe I have been able to organize the book as both a report on his activities and an expression of his personal perspective on those activities.

I believe most people have felt a distressing change in the social atmosphere in Japan today. We see the bond connecting people with each other weakening. Trying to find measures to solve this problem is an urgent matter, and it is not only a concern for journalists, but for society as a whole. People point out the importance of personal interaction, but it is difficult to find an effective way to promote it. In this unhappy and frustrating situation, I find Mr. Yasuda's Go program an indispensable answer.

I have written newspaper articles about Mr. Yasuda's activities, but it is a special honor to be given the opportunity to edit this book. I'd like to thank all the people who willingly offered help and cooperation despite their busy schedules. These people enthusiastically encouraged me, and I owe them a great deal. I would also like to express special thanks to Mr. Teruo Nakagawa of Tosho-bunka, the publisher, for his deep understanding of this interactive Go program, and for his encouragement, effort, and help.

Takeshi Yokouchi
January 2000

Now it's your turn!

Would you like to give this amazing game a try?
Then let's go!

As you have read, it does not take much. If you still
feel to wish support, feel free to contact us or a Go
Association refering to this book. We will help you
or provide ideas and contacts.

BOARD N'STONES